DIVINE PLAYBOOK

DIVINE PLAYBOOK

The Christian's Path to Success, Financial Freedom, and Fulfillment

KEVIN B. PYLES

Copyrighted Material

The Divine Playbook: The Christian's Path to Success, Financial Freedom, and Fulfillment

Copyright © 2020 by Kevin B. Pyles and Christian House Publishing. All Rights Reserved.

No part of this publication may be reproduced, stored in a retrieval system or transmitted, in any form or by any means—electronic, mechanical, photocopying, recording or otherwise—without prior written permission from the publisher, except for the inclusion of brief quotations in a review.

For information about this title or to order other books and/or electronic media, contact the publisher:

Christian House Publishing
KevinBPyles.com
info@KevinBPyles.com

ISBNs:
978-1-7360551-2-0 (hardcover)
978-1-7360551-0-6 (softcover)
978-1-7360551-1-3 (eBook)

Printed in the United States of America

DEDICATION

This is more than a book. It is my life's practice, that forever changed my destiny. As with any life, it would not be possible without people. Although there are many people I would like to thank, there are some that must be mentioned here.

Thank you . . .

To my children, Carmen, Kage, and Kaleah, for giving me joy beyond belief and for being the reason I started this project. You will do much greater things than I.

To my wife, for always being by my side, your unwavering support during the climb, and your unconditional love then and now. I could have never done it without you.

To my mother, for never giving up, while having to be a mother and a father. I know how hard it must have been.

To Rob King, for your invaluable friendship, advice, and mentorship. I will always be grateful.

To Jerry Simpkins, for truly teaching me about Jesus and baptizing my family and me.

To Richard Guidetti, for believing in me when I was a young man in a low place, your invaluable friendship, exposing me to a world I had never seen, always telling me like it is, and helping me get my start. I can never repay you.

TABLE OF CONTENTS

INTRODUCTION		ix
PRELUDE: DEFINING THE GAME		xiii
Chapter 1	LOVE	1
Chapter 2	GRATITUDE	13
Chapter 3	CONFIDENCE	17
Chapter 4	BELIEFS	35
Chapter 5	CLARITY	51
Chapter 6	LEVERAGE	61
Chapter 7	GOALS	67
Chapter 8	GETTING REAL	79
Chapter 9	FOCUS	85
Chapter 10	GET DECISIVE	97
Chapter 11	ACTION	107
Chapter 12	TIME MASTERY	113

Chapter 13 HABITS	141
Chapter 14 COMMUNICATION	149
Chapter 15 HEALTH	161
Chapter 16 GRIT	181
Chapter 17 GIVING	189
Chapter 18 CELEBRATE	195
Chapter 19 FINAL THOUGHTS	201
ABOUT THE AUTHOR	203

INTRODUCTION

Do you feel there has to be a better way? Are you tired, confused, and mentally worn-out? Do you feel like you have tried everything and just cannot catch a break? Are you doing well, but just cannot break through to that next level? Do you know God wants greatness for you, but just haven't quite figured out how?

I was there. That was me. At 17 years old, I found myself living in an 8 x 10 camper without power or running water. It was in this despair that I realized that I was missing something big. Something that would allow me to better myself and live a life that I could respect and be proud of. It was in this humbling solitude that I started reading and studying everything related to success that I could get my hands on. I was not leaning on God in the beginning, but rather, thought I was going it alone. It was me against the world. This was a very trying time in my life. My life could have easily gone directions that would have resulted in an unfulfilled life. I desperately tried to sort through the vast amounts of information out there and implement the plans to the best of my ability. As I began to dig out of the hole I was in, I realized several things:

1. None of the programs seemed to be complete; meaning they did not ensure success and happiness combined.

2. All the programs took way too long to realize results.

3. None of the success programs even mentioned my soul, which was lost and priority one.

4. Most of the programs were way too long, with too much unnecessary information.

5. Many programs lacked the specific actions to take.

As I began to get my act together and change my attitude, so changed my life. I started achieving more and more success. I continued to study and learn through relentless trial and error. I started influencing many around me, and my friends noticed I was changing for the better.

No matter what I was achieving, though, I still had a deep burning feeling that something was missing. It was with the death of my grandfather that I truly gave my life over to Christ. Not part of it, but all of it, and on that day everything changed. Over the next months and years, all the missing pieces began to appear. The voids in my life were gone, and I knew what my destiny was. The Bible became my blueprint, and the more I studied it, the more I wanted to get quiet with God. The more

I got quiet with God, the more He revealed to me. This biblical wisdom and real-life experience merged and led to successes beyond my wildest expectations.

I wrote this book for two reasons. First, I knew what it felt like to touch the bottom. I knew what it felt like to be ashamed of your life. I knew what it felt like to not want to look people in the eye. With young kids of my own, I vowed I would never let this be their experience. I wanted to be sure that if anything ever happened to me before I had the chance to teach them, that I would leave them all the knowledge and experience I had gained. I wanted this information to be in one place with easy-to-follow instructions. The second reason is that once you see and experience magnificent results, and you see how different life can be, you cannot help but want to share it. Everyone has success in them. Whether they believe it or not, it is there.

You are getting ready to embark on a divine journey, resulting in a life you never imagined possible. You are the one that was meant to read this book.

It is your divine destiny!

> **MARK 12:28–29:** *"Of all of the commandments, which is most important?" "The most important one," answered Jesus, "is this: 'Hear, O Israel: The Lord our God, the Lord is one. Love the Lord your God with all your heart and with all your soul and with all your mind and with all your strength.'"*

The information in this book will not change your life; however, you will change your life after reading it. The success already resides within you, and this book will give you a biblical step-by-step action plan to discover, implement, and constantly improve the things necessary to reach your wildest dreams. I can say this because I have done this in my own life, and helped hundreds of others improve their lives as well.

For thousands of years, God's word has held the secret philosophies and concepts needed to produce a successful and happy life. I have taken these philosophies and broken them down into actionable plays for you to run in your own life. I have studied, implemented, and improved these plays for over 30 years, and it is with this plethora of experience that I compose this playbook. God's goal is to have His followers live a life of success and abundance. Heaven will be amazingly blissful, but we can have bliss during our test on Earth, if we get out of God's way.

I chose to name this book *The Divine Playbook* because I wanted you, the reader, to know God's Word must govern strategy, and there must be an action involved. You must run the plays. Could you imagine a football team having a great playbook with all the best plays, but never actually running them? Instead, they just sit and talk about the plays? This sounds hard to imagine, yet it happens in people's lives all the time. Many people know some of what to do, but they just cannot seem to get it done. This book will change that!

> *"A playbook is not only a book of knowledge but also it is a book of action."*
> —Kevin Pyles

PRELUDE:
DEFINING THE GAME

Now that we have discussed why you should read and act on the information in this book, it is imperative that we define the fundamental elements that drive this book and create the core knowledge that you will use throughout your success journey.

DEFINING SUCCESS:
Two scriptures should be kept at the forefront of your success journey.

> **MATTHEW: 16:26:** *What good will it be for someone to gain the whole world, yet forfeit their soul?*

Never forget that the number-one goal of any success plan should be salvation! If you accomplish everything but miss that, then it was all for nothing.

PROVERBS 9:10: *The fear of the Lord is the beginning of wisdom and knowledge of the Holy One is understanding.*

It is imperative that the Lord be first in your life, and that you are pursuing His will. By putting God first, all wisdom and understanding will assuredly be yours.

I am assuming that most people have purchased this book to better themselves, their family, and their lives in some form or fashion. So, the first thing you must do is to define success, and you cannot do that effectively without thinking of first, eternity, and then worldly matters. Success is different for everyone, and you need to be very specific in defining it for yourself. You may have heard the saying there is nothing worse than climbing a ladder only to realize at the top that it is propped up against the wrong house. In other words, you do not want to strive for someone else's goals. Your goals need to be your own.

We will be defining success in detail in chapter 5. I want you to wait until chapter 5 to define success, because you may need to do some "inner-house cleaning" first. I want you to be on the same page with God before you define success.

Defining Principles: Principles are your guiding fundamentals, derived from God's Word. Principles are ideas and actions that you can apply across a broad range of scenarios and situations. The principles in this book will provide you with a new success philosophy that will guide your day-to-day decisions and subsequent actions. Each chapter will start with the scripture it is derived from, followed by a quote to ponder.

Defining Quotes: I love quotes, and after reading this book, you will believe me! Quotes are small golden nuggets of knowledge

PRELUDE: DEFINING THE GAME

that you can read in less than ten seconds, even though it may have taken the writer a lifetime of study to formulate the quote. The thing about quotes is they challenge you to ponder. You can read one quickly, but then think on it for weeks, months, and even years. I have read quotes that have literally changed my life. You will find a quote to ponder at the beginning of each chapter, just after each scripture.

Defining Metaphors: A metaphor is a word or phrase regarded as representative or symbolic of something else, especially something abstract. I believe people can grasp a concept quicker if they relate it to something they already understand. This causes you to paint a picture which will cause the concepts to stick much faster.

Defining Plays: Plays in this book are action items. Plays are where you will take your new knowledge and apply it to your life. Or, as my grandmother used to say, "Where the rubber meets the road!"

Barriers to success: Barriers to success are like fouls; they are the things that can take you out of the game or cause you to lose the game. Barriers are not to be focused on; however, you must be aware of them. Jack Welsh, famed General Electric CEO, was noted as saying that he would not hire any top-level manager who hadn't had at least one major failure. He said he did this because he believed someone who had never failed would not spot the next big failure that could be lurking around the corner.

Defining Scoreboard: The scoreboard is where you will evaluate, score, and record how you are performing in the short-, middle-, and long-term. This is done to ensure you are consistently doing the things that are causing you to win the game and also identifying things that are either neutral or negative, thereby causing you to have setbacks or potentially lose the game.

I tried to keep this book as short as possible while being 100 percent sure that it covers absolutely everything you need to win. Experience has taught me that more information usually is not better, but concise, understandable, and actionable information is!

My main goal is to make this book easy to understand and implement, but do not let that fool you. Although it is designed to be easy to read, the ability to take consistent, sustainable, purposeful action can be quite challenging at times; however, is very achievable if you stick to running the plays.

You must commit to reading this book in its entirety. It has been said before that less than 10 percent of people who start a book make it past the first chapter. I do not really care if this is true as long as you don't become that statistic. Read the book!

I usually start my seminars or consultations with two questions which help people overcome reservations. It will be important to rid yourself of any reservations you may have about this book, so let us start with the same two questions:

1. Would you agree if you do not have everything you want right now, in all aspects of your life, then there is something you do not know?

2. Would you agree, when starting a new endeavor, that it would be faster and easier if you had a plan and guidance

PRELUDE: DEFINING THE GAME

from someone who has already been successful in that endeavor?

If you agree with both statements, then you are ready. As I write this, I already feel the excitement that new success brings. This is the last time you will talk about being successful. The journey has begun, and your success is manifesting!

CHAPTER 1
LOVE

MARK 12:31: *"Love your neighbor as yourself; there is no commandment greater than these."*

1 CORINTHIANS 13:4–8: *Love is patient, love is kind. It does not envy, it does not boast, it is not proud. It does not dishonor others, it is not self-seeking, it is not easily angered, it keeps no record of wrongs. Love does not delight in evil but rejoices with truth. It always trusts, always hopes, always perseveres. Love never fails.*

JOHN 13:34: *"A new command I give you: Love one another. As I have loved you, so you must love one another. By this everyone will know that you are my disciples, if you love one another."*

1 Corinthians 13: 1–3: *If I speak in the tongues of men or of angels, but do not have love, I am only a resounding gong or a clanging symbol. If I have the gift of prophecy and can fathom all mysteries and all knowledge, and if I have a faith that can move mountains, but do not have love, I am nothing. If I give all I possess to the poor and give over my body to hardship that I may boast, but do not have love, I gain nothing.*

Matthew 22: 36–40: *"Teacher, which is the greatest commandment in the Law?" Jesus replied: "Love the Lord your God with all your heart and with all your soul and with all your mind. This is the first and greatest commandment. And the second is like it: 'Love your neighbor as yourself.' All of the Law and the Prophets hang on these two commandments."*

*"Love and compassion are necessities, not luxuries.
Without them, humanity cannot survive."*
—the Dalai Lama

Scripture tells us plainly the importance of love in our lives, and it gives us a clear priority. I do not think happiness and success can exist without the presence of love. Remember, we defined success as having the component of happiness and not just making money. There are plenty of people who make money but are terribly lonely, and would not meet our definition of success. Here are six priorities of love:

CHAPTER I: LOVE

1. Love God

2. Love yourself

3. Love others

4. Love nature

5. Love your time

6. Love what you do

LOVE GOD

Loving God must be the most important, because without his salvation all your works will be in vain. Without love for God, contentment will never come. He first loved you so you can love. God loves you just as you are. An unconditional love. A perfect love. The world cannot replace this love, though it's been trying for thousands of years. God's love is the template for all other love. Love God above all else, and happiness and assurance will always be yours.

LOVE YOURSELF

You must love yourself before you can love others. This may be a challenge for you. One of the biggest reasons for this is because you know yourself well. You are aware of all your shortcomings and all your faults. The mistake here is that you compare your "inner self" with the "outer self" of others. This often causes negative feelings toward yourself. You must look beyond that and lay those faults and burdens at the feet of Jesus. You were made in the image of Christ, and if you have been saved, then you are forgiven and born anew. Any weakness, whether perceived or real, will only reveal God's strength.

What a powerful message. Let God's power shine through your weakness. Stay focused on all your positive attributes and embrace ones you want to work on. It is okay that you're not perfect. No one is. You are just as God made you, and with Him you can grow into what you are supposed to be; that starts with loving yourself. Any shortcomings are only there to make you into who you are to become. Once you have learned to love yourself, only then can you truly love others. Trying to love others while not loving yourself is like spitting in the wind. It does not work, and it will derail you on your path to success.

LOVE OTHERS

JOHN 15:9–10: *"As the Father has loved me, so I have loved you. Now remain in my love. If you keep my commands, you will remain in my love, just as I have kept my Father's commands and remain in His love."*

You are much more valuable than you think. There are many lives that would be negatively affected without you. Current lives, as well as lives that you've yet to encounter. I know some of you have been hurt by worldly love. I suspect we all have at some point, but that should not stop us from loving again. That is the great thing about having the teachings of Jesus to learn from. Jesus gave us the perfect example,

CHAPTER 1: LOVE

in that He showed love even to those who crucified Him. If we follow His example and learn to love even those who hurt us, it will not even be a bump in the road. We will just keep moving forward. I know this is easier said than done, and may be impossible if it just relied on you alone. But with you and God, it can and will happen.

Love is your most powerful emotion and it can literally take you over. I remember reading in one of the Christian study programs that love for a spouse must change and mature; you can't expect to stay in the initial phases of love forever. I had never thought of it, but it makes perfect sense. When you first fall in love, it is all you think about. You think about the person while at work, at play, and at rest. Could you imagine if you were trapped in that stage of love forever? You can kiss success goodbye, because you wouldn't be able to get anything done. All your energy and creativity would be gobbled up. You must move forward into a deeper and more mature love. Many marriages are ruined over this. You must never compare a mature love with the feelings of a sprouting potential love, because they are two totally different things. You can only compare a past sprouting love to a new sprouting love. Love is enduring and battle-tested, so stay the course and let love see you through.

It is especially important, as will be mentioned in our chapter on communication, to learn how to express love to different people. You must show love to someone in the way that they view love and not the way you view it, and this will be different for everyone. Of course, there are general acts of love that would usually be accepted as such, but for your inner circle, you need to know what love means to them. If you are keeping those around you full of love, then they will, in turn, keep you full of love, which allows you to perform at your best.

The key takeaway here is that it starts with you. As God first loved you, you must first love to be loved back. Love keeps you motivated, gives you grit, and will keep you from growing weary. My wife and kids have been my rock all along, and without their love and support it would have been much more difficult to climb the mountain of success. Loving others is imperative to success. People can sense genuine love and they respond to it. They are drawn to it, they follow it, they fight for it, and they stand by it.

LOVE NATURE

For this writing, when I say "nature," I am referring to anything physical outside yourself. The earth, animals, the sun, the moon, the air, etc. It is important to love nature. Without it, you wouldn't have to worry about success, now would you? Could you make a living and become successful floating in outer space? You have been delivered to the perfect place, at a perfect time, with just the right circumstances for success. You should be in awe of nature, just like you should be in awe of yourself.

When I say love nature I do not just mean being a good steward of resources, although that is extremely important and should go without saying. I mean to deeply connect with nature. The Word that created you also created it. It is the same Word! Get in nature as much as you can and observe it, get fascinated by it, and learn from it. There are many lessons to be learned from nature, if you slow down and pay attention. I think God speaks and teaches us through nature.

CHAPTER 1: LOVE

Let us look at a few examples. Look at the oak tree. The acorn does not fight its destiny. From that tiny acorn will grow a mighty tree. The roots seek out their needed water and nutrients. The leaves reach out to praise the sun. It does not get in its own way; it just lets God's will be done. Remember the parable Jesus told about the birds not storing away in barns, but they were always provided for? And then He asked, "Are you not more valuable than they?" Birds awaken with the day, singing in praise. They don't wake up, kick a leaf, and say, "Dag-gone-it! I don't want to get up today!" Only we do that. The rooster does not procrastinate with his daybreak crow. Only we do that. The plants don't worry about the next rain, but wait patiently in expectancy. Only we, as humans, worry and live in haste. Get in nature, be quiet, and start learning its valuable lessons.

LOVE TIME

We discuss time in detail in another chapter, but it is important to note a simple principle here. You need to love your time. Every year, month, week, day, minute, and second. Life is created and lost in a second of time. Your life can change in the blink of an eye, so you need to love all of it. You can change your life for the better in the second that you decide to change it.

LOVE WHAT YOU DO

You should work toward doing something that you love even if you cannot quite start there. I think some people try to get there a little too soon. Just follow God's plan. It may be that what you love, at least successfully, requires a greater skill set than what you currently have. You may need more life experience before doing what you love becomes your career. Sometimes you need to generate income, save, and then work toward doing what you love. Doing what you love takes two things: thought and time. It can be difficult to know what you love to do at first, but you can find it through thought and time. Look for common themes in multiple things that you love to do. For example: I am a physical therapist, a martial arts teacher, a Sunday school teacher, a business owner, and a motivational speaker. I like all those things but what I really love to do is to lead and help people live their best life. Each of the things that I do has that component, and that is why I enjoy doing them. I found, over the years, that the more people I can help, the more enjoyment I experience. That is one of the reasons that I wrote this book.

CHAPTER I: LOVE

PLAY 1

LOVE

1. Assess your love for God by praying and talking with Him daily. Ask for love to govern all that you do.

2. Practice loving yourself. Write down your three best qualities and place them beside your bed. Read them aloud to yourself, saying, "I love you [your name] because [state your quality here]." Do this for each quality. Perform this when you first wake up in the morning, and right before you go to bed at night. If this feels awkward, then it just shows that you need practice in this area, because loving yourself should come naturally.

3. Create sticky notes about why you love yourself and put them on your vanity mirror, on the fridge, in your car, at your desk, etc. You only need to do this until you feel a deep love for yourself.

4. Set a reminder on your phone to remember these positive attributes, and that you love yourself.

5. Practice loving others.
    a. **Inner circle.** Find out what love means to those in your inner circle. Write down and then list things

that you can do that would demonstrate love to them. This could be things like buying a gift and card for no reason, or doing a chore they would normally have to do themselves, or asking them if they need to vent while you sit and listen. I think you get the point. Be sure to read, *The Five Love Languages*, by Gary Chapman!

    b. **Outer circle.** Your outer circle is everyone that is not in your inner circle. Start a temporary love journal. Each week, I want you to do one random act of kindness for someone and record that in your love journal. This can be as simple as holding a door for someone or making an unexpected phone call. It could be as elaborate as throwing a party for someone or some group for no reason other than to show them they are loved. For example, you might throw a special party for the kids at the local foster home. You can be creative here; the sky is the limit.

6. Love nature. Get in nature more. Try to do something in nature at least once per quarter. If you can do more often, you should. Just take a little notepad and informally jot down things you observe in nature. It could be that you notice how God provides for each animal and they have just what they need. It could be the sheer majesty of the sun setting over a mountain ridge and the realization of how small your problems are for God.

CHAPTER I: LOVE

7. Love what you do. Write down what you would do if money did not matter. Look at past and current jobs to see if you can find that common theme that you enjoyed in them. You may find that what you thought you loved to do is not the job itself, but there is a theme hidden within it that you love.

CHAPTER 2
GRATITUDE

PHILIPPIANS 4:6: *Do not be anxious about anything, but in every situation, by prayer and petition with thanksgiving, present your request to God.*

HEBREWS 12:28: *Therefore, since we are receiving a kingdom that cannot be shaken, let us be thankful, and so worship God acceptably with reverence and awe.*

1 THESSALONIANS 5:16–18: *Rejoice always, pray continually, give thanks in all circumstances for this is God's will for you in Jesus Christ.*

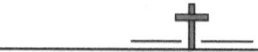

> *"The hardest arithmetic to master is that which enables a man to count his own blessings."*
> —Eric Hoffer, American philosopher and writer

> *"Gratitude is to fear as a base is to acid."*
> —Kevin Pyles

Let us define gratitude. Gratitude is an emotional state of acknowledgment and appreciation of a benefit that one has or will receive, that they did nothing to deserve. I have found in my life that gratitude has allowed me to face many challenges and overcome many obstacles. Gratitude serves two main purposes: The first is to remove all fear, and that is so important on your quest for success. I must note here that fear is one of the main reasons that people abandon their dreams and do not accomplish what they had set out to do. Fear of failure, fear of looking dumb, fear of the unknown, fear of losing money or respect, fear of succeeding and not being able to handle it. Fear has probably derailed more lives from success and happiness than TV, social media, and video games combined—and that is a lot!

In my opinion, fear cannot exist in the presence of gratitude; that is precisely why I start every single day with a healthy dose of gratitude. This single strategy has allowed me to make many scary decisions that were necessary to get me to where I am today.

CHAPTER 2: GRATITUDE

Without practicing gratitude first, I probably would not have been able to overcome the fear of making those decisions. If I know I have a big decision to make I do two things: a session of gratitude and a session of total quiet time with God; and you should do this too.

The second purpose of gratitude is happiness. Happiness is nothing more than a state of mind, and being grateful is a great way to foster happiness. We simply perform better when we are happy. It is easy to get caught up in pity parties of your own or drawn into other peoples', which can sidetrack you. Research has shown that the fastest way to happiness is through the regular practice of gratitude. Dr. Emmons, a leading gratitude researcher, did a study where participants were to keep a gratitude journal for just three weeks. Prior to beginning the journal, they were given a happiness assessment. After journaling their gratitude for three weeks, they repeated the assessment, and the results reflected a whopping 25 percent increase in perceived happiness. That is 25 percent in only three weeks, and that increase lasted for three months after they stopped journaling.

That is impressive enough by itself, but that's not all. The researchers also gave an assessment to the participants' closest friends, asking them to rate the participant. The friends also rated a 25 percent increase in the participants' happiness. In other words, the friends of the participants also noticed how much happier their friend seemed after three weeks of gratitude journaling. These findings are in line with numerous studies; we all should take note!

Play 2

GRATITUDE

1. Start a gratitude journal. Keep the journal beside your bed, so you see it every day.

   Each morning write down three things that you are grateful for.

2. Practice gratitude in your morning vision quest ritual (covered later in this book).

   If you are in a place where you can do this out loud, then do so. The louder you are and the more emotion you create, the better!

3. Any time you are feeling down or defeated, or are being derailed by fear, take a few minutes to read through your gratitude journal.

CHAPTER 3
CONFIDENCE

2 Timothy 1:7: *For God hath not given us the spirit of fear: but of power, and of love, and of a sound mind.*

Philippians 4:13: *I can do all things through Christ who strengthens me.*

Joshua 1:9: *Have not I commanded thee? Be strong and of a good courage; be not afraid, neither be dismayed: for the Lord thy God is with thee whithersoever thou goest.*

> "To succeed in life, you need two things: ignorance and confidence."
> —Mark Twain

> "Each man carries in his eyes the exact position on his rank."
> —Ralph Waldo Emerson

Confidence is the belief of being certain that one can rely on someone, something, or himself. I believe confidence is the most elusive of all principles in this book, and could arguably be the most important. That is right, the lack of belief in yourself may be the single greatest detriment to your success. This is what is great about being a Christian. You don't have to wait until you develop confidence in yourself, because God tells you in His Word that your confidence need only to lie in Him, and He will provide all that you need.

I love the wittiness in Mark Twain's quote above. He is basically saying all you need is ignorance, meaning you do not know what you don't know, and confidence, the belief that you can do anything. Obviously, I think there is more to it, but this is the right direction. I think the reason that confidence is so elusive is because it resides in the subconscious mind, but is often analyzed in the conscious mind. A good example is someone who constantly boasts on how good they are at something when deep down they are really scared and doubt themselves. I am sure you have heard the term "wearing a mask." People present one image to the public, but live another inside their own head. It is like they are trying to convince themselves as much as they are trying to convince their peers. I firmly believe that the earlier in life you build confidence or belief in yourself, the easier it is

CHAPTER 3: CONFIDENCE

to use it; however, I am living proof that you can build it at any point in life, with the right tools.

Another thing that makes confidence and self-esteem so tricky is that you can have it in one area and still lack it in another. The key is to build your confidence within the areas necessary for you to achieve your goals. Confidence is like a muscle. The more you work it out the bigger it gets. Just like strength, you can gain or lose confidence at any time. The nature of confidence is that it builds up slow, but can break down fast, much like strength. This can cause major problems on your journey to success if the proper strategies are not put in place. In my martial arts academy, we have a motto for our youth program that reads "Arm your child with self-esteem." We say that because we know that one little principle can affect so many other variables in a child's life. It is impossible to prepare a child for everything they will face in their life, but if you have armed them with self-esteem, the chances of them coming out on top of any situation go way up.

"A strong self-esteem will free action, while fear paralyzes it."
—Kevin Pyles

You can find a good example of this with dogs. If you take two puppies from the same litter and put one of them in a home that continually scolds, hits, and kicks at the puppy, he will become a nervous shell of himself that will barely look you in the eye. Conversely, if you take the other pup and put him in a loving home that enrolls him in protection training, he will most certainly grow into a formidable animal that would most likely stand his ground.

Of course, there are always genetic dispositions, but the point is still a valid one. Some people are fortunate to have confidence strategically instilled in them as kids by a parent, coach, or other mentor. But what about the people that did not have these experiences, or worse yet had experience that lessened their confidence. Is there hope? Absolutely! As we said earlier, confidence can be gained or lost at any time.

Did you know that in 1923, when Babe "The Bambino" Ruth set the home run record and the record for the highest batting average, that he also struck out more than any other player? See, you must be willing to swing for the fences and risk striking out in order to get the home run. I believe that most people sell themselves short, at least on the inside. They may have a good mask for the outside, but on the inside, they are often fearful and anxious. This often happens because they think their failures are unique to them, but that is simply not true.

One of the best ways to convince yourself of this fact is by reading biographies of people that you respect. Maybe it is someone who accomplished great things. You will quickly find that their lives were often filled with failures. In fact, most of the time they fail more than they succeed, but the critical point is that they refused to give up. Once you accept this as fact and embed it in your subconscious mind, you will never be the same. Your ability to act will increase drastically. One of the most important beliefs that you need to adopt is this: You must believe that if you have a failure, it was the situation that failed and not you. You are always a winner who may have situations that fail, but you are not a failure!

When I first got into business as a young, green entrepreneur with zero formal business education, I would meet with powerful

CHAPTER 3: CONFIDENCE

CEOs and assume they had something or knew something I did not, but that really was not the case. They were in a different circumstance than me, but that is it. They were not better than me. What many of them did have was confidence, because they had experience.

One of my favorite reads was about George Washington and the American Revolution. He had so many reasons to throw in the towel and quit, but he would not. He managed to stay the course and gain the respect of nearly all his peers. It is important to know that just because you have confidence, it doesn't mean that you will never question yourself, because you will, as do all great achievers. The difference is how you answer those questions and your belief in those answers!

Some of the best work that I have seen on the power of the self-image is that of Dr. Maxwell Malt, plastic surgeon. Dr. Malt's research demonstrated that the self-image is deeply rooted, and that often, a surgery to enhance someone's physical appearance had negligible effect on how they viewed themselves. In other words, he realized that patients who had a low self-image because of a physical blemish did not see the positive change after the surgery, because their thought processes were governed by an embedded low self-image.

It is possible to be confident in some areas and not in others. You can probably see this at work in your own life. This is why it is so important to build confidence in areas that will directly affect your success. I think confidence can be taught and instilled, but it seems to be instilled at a deeper level by positive experiences or successful outcomes. It is much easier to have confidence in yourself to run a marathon after you have run your first one.

One of the most important concepts when trying to build confidence is to determine whether you have a growth mindset or a fixed mindset. Mindset is a simple idea popularized by world-renowned Stanford University psychologist Carol Dweck, through decades of research on achievement and success. If you are not familiar with her work, you should look her up. Through years of research, she found that people generally have one of two mindsets: growth, whereby they believed that they could improve at a thing; or fixed, whereby they believed that they were born with attributes they were stuck with for life and could not improve upon.

You learn through her teachings to reward and focus on the process, and not so much the outcome. Doing this allows you to separate yourself somewhat from the result and simply focus on improving your preparation. I always tell my athletes that the outcome only defines that situation, and that it does not define them. What defines them is their effort and discipline in preparing. You can never fail with this thought process, because you can always learn, grow, and improve.

You should stop and take some time to reflect here. This is a life-altering belief system. A good example of this is tying your shoes. Most people past seven years of age can tie their own shoes; however, most people failed miserably at this little endeavor when they first tried it. Had they quit, they would still be tripping over their shoelaces in their twenties, but most parents will not let their children quit trying until they get it. As kids get older, they can tie their shoes while standing on one foot and talking on the phone! Do you see the irony here? Parents know that if their kids keep trying long enough, despite multiple failed

CHAPTER 3: CONFIDENCE

attempts that their kids will eventually tie their shoes, yet those same parents may give up on their adult dreams because of a few failed attempts. Success leaves clues, if you know where to look for them.

Complete this sentence: Practice makes [_____].

Most people are taught at an early age to say perfect, but you should not. Practice makes improvement. I guess you could say I learned this the hard way. When I was young, I thought that I always had to be perfect at whatever I did. Although this did make me work hard, it put an unrealistic pressure on me that eventually caught up with me. As human beings, we can always improve. That is the belief system that you should adopt. Research has demonstrated that someone focused on getting better will almost always outperform someone who is focused on being perfect. If you are focused on being the best, then every time you are not the best, your confidence takes a hit, and fear will eventually paralyze you from doing the things you need to do. If you choose to focus on improving, then you will always either win or learn!

As you build your confidence you will become more efficient. I now make decisions in minutes that it used to take me a week to make. Another great way to self-build your confidence is through "transference." Transference is where you take a difficult situation that you made it through in your past and transfer that confidence and success to a present-day problem. If you accomplished that then, then you can accomplish this now. For example, if you lost a job ten years ago, learned a whole new craft, and started a new career, then you have the focus and discipline to do the things you need to do to start your own company, today.

Many people might look at Lucille Ball of the *I Love Lucy* show, and think, I wished I had pursued acting! But it has been said that drama instructors urged her to try another profession. Lucille Ball refused to believe this. Can you imagine getting rejection from the people tasked with teaching you and still believing in yourself? Now that is a deep-rooted believe system! She let the rejection define that situation, but she never let it define her. Ray Kroc had a similar story: Going from a milkshake-mixer salesman to buying and leading McDonalds, one of the most successful franchises in the world. He also owned the San Diego Padres for about ten years, until his death in 1984.

Here is another example. Read this list of setbacks, and just think to yourself when you would have thrown in the towel.

- Lost his job
- Defeated for legislature
- Failed business venture
- Sweetheart died
- Had nervous breakdown
- Defeated for speaker
- Defeated for Congress
- Elected to Congress only to lose renomination
- Rejected for land officer
- Defeated for Senate
- Defeated for nomination as vice president
- Defeated for Senate again

Seriously, would you have had the confidence to try anything at this point?

CHAPTER 3: CONFIDENCE

Well Abraham Lincoln did, and he was elected president in 1860!

This underscores my point about reading biographies. There are extremely powerful lessons hiding within the pages of biographies. Once you realize that nearly all people of great accomplishment had many, many failures on the way to where they wanted to be, you will be able to apply that belief system to your own life.

"My lack of experience has allowed me to fail my way to success."
—Kevin Pyles

One of my favorite quotes is below.

"Success comes from good judgment . . .
Good judgment comes from experience . . .
Experience comes from bad judgment."
—Anthony Robbins

A great way to build confidence is through training your subconscious mind. Your subconscious mind is so powerful and plays a major role in your success or lack thereof. Your ability to use your subconscious mind will be in direct relation of your understanding of its principles and the application of them. Your subconscious mind is just like the soil, in that it will accept any kind of seed that you plant. It does not matter if that seed is a vegetable that would benefit you or a poisonous plant that would harm you. It simply accepts the seed and starts to grow it.

I believe your subconscious mind holds your true self-image while your conscious mind holds the mask that is put forward to the world. The subconscious mind may be one of the most overlooked areas when dealing with success, but there is simply no way to talk about winning or success without learning the role that the subconscious mind plays. I've literally seen hundreds of people that have won half the battle by having a good game plan, great written goals, etc., but because they never addressed the role of their subconscious mind, they simply fell short, time after time. Think of your conscious mind like a keyboard that you use to write programs and your subconscious mind as the program that runs in the background. In other words, you can build a program that computes complex math equations, but you must key in how the program is to run for it to give you the answers. The neat thing is that once the program is running you do not have to know how to solve the complex problems, because the program will do it for you.

Programming the subconscious mind for confidence takes some time. Some of you may be reversing a lifetime of confidence-breaking programming. I believe there are six important strategies to implement here. They are 1) prayer, 2) visualizations, 3) the mirror method, 4) incantations, 5) external affirmations, and 6) acting. Your subconscious mind does not know the difference between real and imaginary. This is especially useful information because it allows you to program advantageously.

Prayer. You've probably heard the scripture of Matthew 7:7: "Ask and it will be given to you; seek and you will find, knock and the door will be opened to you." Each morning, you should pray for God to manifest Himself through you. To deliver you into your divine destiny. Pray for God's strength to shine through

CHAPTER 3: CONFIDENCE

your weakness. Ask for God to lead, guide, and direct all that you do, and then believe it has been done!

Visualization. In my opinion, this is one of the strongest forms of programming for the subconscious mind. In this case, a picture really is worth a thousand words. Images stick in your brain and send powerful messages throughout your body. For example, if you are having a bad dream where you are being chased, you will wake up sweating and with your heart pounding, even though you were doing nothing more than lying in your bed.

Try doing something similar while you are awake. It is much more difficult, because your conscious mind will keep interrupting. Making a short mind-movie of yourself, as you want yourself to be, is a great way to influence and program your subconscious mind. It is important to see yourself as confident and successful in your mind-movie. With practice and consistency your "mental" you will begin manifesting externally. Said differently, you will begin to become the person you picture in your head. Everything you are has been created first within your mind, whether intentionally or unintentionally.

When you create this mind-movie, be sure to include scenes that prove you have reached your goals. For example, if you want to lose weight, then in the movie, picture yourself coming home from work and walking through the door as the person you want to be. If you do this regularly and with lots of emotion, your subconscious mind will see this as real and help ensure that you do the things that need to be done to get you to that weight. You will begin to feel and act like the person you desire to be.

The Mirror Mantra. When I first learned of the mirror mantra, I thought it a bit trite. I felt looking in the mirror could not be of much value, but I always test new strategies before discarding them. As I started to practice, I remembered a valuable lesson I learned from a Korean Grandmaster. He had a drill where we would sit on our knees across from another person and do nothing but look into their eyes. This was an uncomfortable drill for most of us. He said the eyes were the gateway to the soul and where our true confidence lies. As we rotated through different partners, you could not only see the different levels of confidence in people, but you could also feel it! When it comes to inner reflection you are the only partner you need and the only one that matters. Here is how it works:

1. Stand in front of a mirror where you can see enough of yourself to read your body language.

2. Take a power breath. Four sharp breaths in, hold two seconds, and then breathe out for six seconds.

3. Stand tall, shoulders back, head up.

4. Look into your eyes and say: "I was made for greatness and will not be denied!"

5. Read your goals to yourself with conviction and emotion. Start each sentence with "I will . . .

6. Say with conviction, "God, lead, guide, and direct my steps and decisions!"

CHAPTER 3: CONFIDENCE

You can also substitute in any statements that are particular to your current struggles or situation.

Incantations. Incantations are groups of words chanted in a magical way. I prefer to use a "catchy" rhythm, because I think it sticks a little quicker. Put the catchy rhythm to the test for yourself. The next time you are around a family member or friend, gently hum or whistle a catchy tune like *The Andy Griffith Show* theme song for a couple minutes. Then monitor them throughout the day. You will most likely notice that they start to hum or whistle the theme, or maybe talk about the show. This demonstrates that their subconscious picked it up. I have done this with my kids several times, and it almost always works (as long as they were not totally zoned out). Remember, they may not do it right away, but just stay aware, and it will come out eventually.

I first realized the true power of incantations after having done them daily for several months. I would catch myself tapping my hand in the rhythm, or humming the rhythm, that I had been using for my incantations. The thing to note here is that I was always in a great mood when I noticed this. The reason my subconscious associated a great mood with the incantations is because I always practice them right after a gratitude session, and with lots of positive emotion. The programs, or the lack of programs, literally molds you into the person you are. If your subconscious is predominately running success-serving programs, then you will become successful. Likewise, if it is running programs rooted in fear, anxiety, or anger, you will live a life of discontent. If your subconscious mind runs certain programs over and over, they eventually become deep-rooted belief systems. You want your deep-rooted belief systems to be success drivers and not success robbers. We will be touching more on belief systems in the next chapter.

External Affirmations. This is a strategy that I discovered by accident. I have always practiced emotional flagging where, when feeling a strong emotion, I pause for a moment to interpret the underlying cause. In this case, I was just returning to the office when I noticed I had missed a call, and had a voice message from my wife. Upon playing the message, I felt invigorated. The message said, "Honey, I just wanted you to know that I believe in you. You will not be denied and will accomplish everything you set your mind on. We are so lucky to have a man like you." I must have listened to that message a thousand times over the next six months. It gave me so much power and energy. Much more power than my own incantations did. My emotional flagging strategy caused me to question why. So, I dug into these strong emotions to find the etiology. After some soul-searching, I realized that as a boy I had great pain associated with my father not being present for me or our family. My father left when I was five years old, and let us down hundreds of times by not keeping his word and not showing up when he said he would. Because of this pain, I had a deep-rooted drive to be a man my wife and kids could count on. Subconsciously, I never wanted my children to feel that pain. I now realize, it is at the very essence of who I am. Hearing my wife say those words totally validated everything I stood for. Realizing that these external affirmations were so beneficial, I knew I must include them in my success strategy.

Through much study and thought I developed a few rules for external affirmations:

CHAPTER 3: CONFIDENCE

1. The deeper your connection with the person the more powerful the result.

2. The affirmations need to be directly supportive of the area that strikes a powerful emotion within you.

3. Benefit can still be derived with messaging from those you do not know but will not be as powerful.

I then had my kids record several affirmations into the memo section of my phone. Doing it this way allowed me to play them anytime I wanted. Here are examples of some that I had my kids do:

- Daddy, I can always count on you.
- I know you are creating a great future for me.
- I know that you will never quit.
- I know you will win and achieve your dreams.

I cannot tell you how many times my wife's and my kids' messages lifted me up, renewed my spirit, and gave me the vigor to stay the course!

Acting. Sometimes you must act your way to the confidence you need. Acting as if you are already who you want to be can have a great effect. You should dress and speak as if the successes have already occurred. Your subconscious will adopt this positive emotion as the real you, and soon it will be.

Here are some common things you can do to act your way to success:

THE DIVINE PLAYBOOK

1. Dress the part.

2. Keep your office and automobile clean and organized.

3. Talk the part. Talk to yourself and others with confidence, projecting success.

4. Keep a little money in your pocket. Just knowing it is there can give you a boost.

5. Act out pretend phone conversations where you are making deals, investing, and "high rolling," so to speak.

6. Have fun with it!

Play 3
CONFIDENCE

1. Make a list of all your good qualities.

2. Make a list of past accomplishments and times that you got through a demanding situation. Use these for transference when needed.

3. Make a list of the skills that you had to have and use to accomplish the things listed in number two.

4. Create your prayer for confidence.

5. Create a mind-movie of about three to five minutes, by writing it out. You will want to do this after you have set your goals, etc. Play your mind-movie two times per day, every day. I like to do this first thing in the morning and right before bed. I will also do this after a situation that did not go well that might have elicited negative emotions. Your mind-movie should be very detailed; the more detailed the better. After all, color movies are more interesting to watch than black-and-white ones. The advanced graphics in today's films are much better than twenty years ago, and are often more exciting because of that. For example, if in your

movie you open a glass door, see the fog on it, and if you sit down, hear the chair squeak. Be sure to see all your goals realized.

6. Implement the mirror mantra as described. Generally, about ten minutes in duration.

7. Create three incantations that are short and rhythmic. Repeat these for five to fifteen minutes, depending on how much time you allow for your morning vision quest. (The morning vision quest will be discussed in the chapter about habits.) Say these loudly, and with as much positive emotion as possible. Make sure these incantations support the attributes that you need to obtain your goals.

8. Create your external affirmations with those who love you most.

9. Act like the who you wish to be each day, and soon you will not be acting!

CHAPTER 4
BELIEFS

Matthew 8:13: And Jesus said unto the centurion, "Go thy way; and as thou hast believed, so be it done unto thee."

Psalms 37:4: Delight thyself also in the Lord; and he shall give thee the desires of thine heart.

Matthew 17:20: And Jesus said unto them, "Because of your unbelief: for verily I say unto you, if ye have the faith as a grain of mustard seed, ye shall say unto this mountain, 'Remove hence to yonder place'; and it shall remove; and nothing shall be impossible unto you."

Psalms 138:8: The Lord will perfect that which concerneth me: thy mercy, O Lord, endureth forever: forsake not the works of thine own hands.

> *"Whether you think you can or think you can't, you are right."*
> —Henry Ford

Ford's statement on belief is a powerful one.

How amazing is the last part of Matthew 17:20? *And nothing shall be impossible unto you.* As a Christian, this should make you jump with joy! If you ask most Christians if they believe every word in the Bible, they will answer, "Yes." The Bible is full of statements about the successful life of believers and notes that Christians should be enjoying the gifts of love, joy, peace, patience, kindness, goodness, faithfulness, gentleness, and self-control. And yet, in many cases, I do not see Christians living any more happily than nonbelievers. This is not the way God intended Christians to live. If you draw near to God, then He will draw near to you, and I believe this will become clear.

Much of the research on success today points to one's belief in self as one of the top determinants of success. In other words, believing that you will succeed has a lot to do with whether you will. You should be rejoicing right now, because this important principle is already residing within you. Belief and confidence work together.

The only problem is that you may have beliefs that are currently derailing you from your success. I think most beliefs start as conscious thoughts, due to statements made by you or someone else; these are eventually adopted by the subconscious

CHAPTER 4: BELIEFS

mind and accepted as beliefs. I also believe that the more emotion that is associated with the conscious thought, the quicker that belief manifests, and the deeper it becomes rooted into the fabric of who you are. It should be noted here that it is not important whether the belief be factual, just that you accept it as true, so be careful.

One example is that of a child that has been abused or shunned by a parent; they will often struggle with self-esteem because of their belief that they are no good, or that it was their fault. When a parent that is supposed to be a protector and mentor is not, it can greatly scar a child due to the emotion involved. If this is never addressed, it can cause a lifetime of problems, often without being understood as the cause. I like to think of thoughts that have been adopted by the subconscious to form a belief as "pillars."

I think of them as pillars because they support who you are. There are pillars which cause you to succeed, and pillars that will cause you to fail. There are two things that make pillars stronger. The first is footings, or the amount of emotion associated with the belief. The second is cure time, or the amount of time the belief has been embedded and reinforced. The stronger the pillar, the more difficult to disrupt, and perhaps the longer it will take to change. Notice I did not say impossible, I simply said longer.

When I was 16 years old, I was driving on a wet road and as I rounded a curve I hydroplaned and spun around in the road about four times, barely missing a telephone pole. This almost scared my passenger and me to death. From then on, I was very apprehensive about driving on wet roads, and I had plenty of emotion anchoring that thought.

Let me clarify that this belief goes beyond the typical thought to slow down a bit when it is raining. This was even worse if I was a passenger with someone else when the roads were wet. These emotions were powerful. It was not until I developed an understanding of beliefs and pillars that I started to correct this exaggerated fear. I remembered that the tires on that car had no tread, and that good tread makes a big difference. I remembered that it was in a curve and a stream of water was running across the road. I worked on this false emotional hijacking for quite some time. Now, although cautious, I have no anxiety associated with wet roads.

Now that you see the relationship that beliefs have with who you are, it is important for us to uncover yours. You may find that your true, deep-rooted pillars are often not what you think they are. Often one confuses what they want to believe, which is produced in their conscious mind with what they actually believe which is housed in their subconscious mind.

So how do you find your true beliefs? I think the first step is to train yourself in what I call "emotional flagging." What I mean is that you must become very sensitive to your emotions. If you hear someone say something and then you feel yourself getting angry, then you need to stop and ask yourself, "Where is this anger coming from or why am I feeling this way?" You need to do this with every emotion, but especially with ones that are not of the fruit of the spirit. These emotions are the warning flags to knowing your true beliefs or pillars. You will soon begin to discover some of the deep-rooted pillars lurking within your subconscious, and derailing you from success.

CHAPTER 4: BELIEFS

You can think of it like this: In the beginning your thoughts develop your beliefs but once beliefs are established, it goes like this:

Beliefs>Thoughts>Emotions>Actions (or lack of) = Result

It is probably safe to assume that many of you have some beliefs that do not serve you well. Most likely this is due to one of two things. Either your parents—directly or indirectly—instilled in you a disserving belief, or interactions with your environment formed the belief. The problem with both is that neither method is usually designed as part of an overall long-term success plan, but rather are more haphazard in design. Do not worry, most of us are in this same boat until we learn how this works.

Most people's beliefs are formed before they are even aware that they have beliefs. Here is a simple example of how we can develop a mistaken belief as a child; my son did this even after being told not to. If a toddler touches a hot stove and burns his hand, he immediately thinks that stoves are bad, because the stove caused him pain. He may want to avoid stoves for quite some time. He does not realize that stoves are very helpful appliances, and it is touching a hot stove burner that is bad. If that toddler never saw another stove in his life, and no one ever taught him otherwise, he would most assuredly live his entire life thinking that stoves were bad.

Now, I know this is a trivial example, but this is how it happens. Another example could be when a child who constantly hears a parent say, "filthy rich." It implies that if someone is rich, then they must be a bad person. Do not laugh, I've known many people who discovered this was one of their problems.

A belief can be formed before you know it. You have an experience that seems to be bad, and your subconscious records the experience along with the associated negative emotions. Your subconscious does not and cannot reason out what exactly caused the negative emotions; it just records what is thought and felt at the time of the event. It will remain this way unless you have a more powerful experience that proves otherwise, or unless you are exposed to knowledge that teaches you to strategically train your subconscious. The first thing you must do is to discover as many of your true beliefs as you can, and then categorize them as serving or disserving to your dreams.

You need to analyze your beliefs in key areas like success, happiness, business, family, relationships, money, a higher power, and people to name a few. It's okay if you can't uncover all your beliefs right away. Just being aware will allow you to discover them, given a little time. The main thing is to not rely on your conscious mind, because often it will tell you what you want to hear, or what you think your belief should be. Your emotions will tell you what your beliefs truly are.

Gautama Buddha put it like this: "We are what we think, all that we are arises with our thoughts, with our thoughts we make our world."

Research has demonstrated that optimism, which is basically a belief, releases powerful endorphins. It is like we sing because we are happy, then we are happy because we sing. Dr. Bernie Siegel has performed studies where people with multiple personalities had an allergy or other disease, that was present with one personality, disappear as the personality changed. This demonstrates the power of the subconscious mind. I believe your brain holds the solution to any obstacle you will ever face. The key is having spent enough time in training to be able to tap into it when needed. As a follower of Jesus, you have a huge bonus in this area: The Holy Spirit. When talking about the Holy Spirit's role in your success I like to reference three scriptures:

> JOHN 14:16–18: *And I will ask the Father, and he will give you another advocate to help you and be with you forever—the Spirit of truth. The world cannot accept him, because it neither sees him nor knows him. But you know him, for he lives with you and will be in you. I will not leave you as orphans; I will come to you.*

> JOHN 14:26: *But the Advocate, the Holy Spirit, whom the Father will send in my name, will teach you all things and will remind you of everything I have said to you.*

> JOHN 16: 7–9: *But very truly I tell you, it is for your good that I am going away. Unless I go away, the Advocate will not come to you; but if I go, I will send him to you. When he comes, he will prove the world to be in the wrong about sin and righteousness and judgment: about sin, because people do not believe in me.*

God's promise to provide us with an advocate to teach us all things is profound. Instead of being left to figure it all out alone, Christians have been anointed with the Holy Spirit to guide and direct us. If you learn to "be still" and know God, His Spirit will guide and direct you in all ways to ensure peace and prosperity.

Your goal is to align your subconscious with the Holy Spirit. Here is an exercise that I performed in a church training that I took part in: Close your eyes and hope that things will turn out okay. Pay close attention to how that makes you feel. Not too great, huh? Now close your eyes and know 100 percent that God is in control and will work all things to your good. As Paul said in Romans 8:28, "And we know that all things work together for good to them that love God, to them who are the called according to his purpose." Oh, how great it is to be a child of God. Surely, you can feel the difference that is generated inside with the prior exercise. Positive beliefs create positive emotions.

Okay, so if you have figured out and identified that you have disserving beliefs, you need to replace them with serving ones. We have already said that beliefs reside in the subconscious mind, so that is where we must change them.

Let us back up and make sure you have the steps:

1. Identify disserving beliefs.

2. Identify what you need the beliefs to be.

3. Systematically impress the new serving belief on the subconscious mind.

Obviously, the third step is where the brunt of the work is going to take place.

It has been said that our conscious and subconscious mind work and see things differently. Much research suggests that the conscious mind can only process about 50 bits per second;

CHAPTER 4: BELIEFS

however, our senses are sending the brain approximately eleven million bits of information per second. So how are our brains dealing with all this information? With the one hundred billion cells in the brain, each with connections to hundreds or thousands of other cells, it could be that the subconscious mind has the ability to process over one hundred billion bits of information per second. That is incredible!

The more we train and impress a conscious thought or activity on the brain, the more it becomes automatic and does not need conscious control. When you continually tell your brain that something is important, the subconscious seems to always be on the search for it. To keep this simple, I will describe it like this: Our brains have a mechanism that acts as a gatekeeper. This gatekeeper looks for information that matches the way we think. If the gatekeeper thinks a piece of information is important, then he picks it out and lets it through. This is why everyone sees the world differently.

This is very much like a search engine on a computer. You enter a piece of information and hit search; then the search engine scans all the available information and picks out what it thinks matches what you are looking for and brings it to the front of the pack, so you can give it your attention. This process is continually going on in your brain, whether you are awake or asleep. This is important, because if you do not create a clear and concise picture of what serves you in accomplishing your dreams, then you are likely to miss critical bits of information.

In my opinion, there are two major concepts at play when dealing with the subconscious mind: building new success-serving beliefs and interrupting nonserving beliefs. I call this "prepping the soil." You cannot grow the thoughts, emotions, and action you need without creating the proper foundation in which for them to grow.

Consider this story: A young man buys some land and wants to put cows on it. He gets the land, puts the cows on it, but they are not gaining weight as they should. He notices that the cattle farm across the road has big, heavy cows. One day, he asks the farmer how his cows do so well. The farmer explains, "Well, son, before I ever put cows on my land, I analyzed the soil to see what the nutrition was. Once I had that assessment, I spent a couple of years getting rid of the bad stuff and building up the soil so it would want to grow the good stuff and not the bad. Once I had the land growing the right forage, I then put my cows on there, and everything has worked great." Just like the farmer's soil, your subconscious must be prepped and rid of the bad, and built up with the good, to foster successful beliefs and actions.

I have found the best way to create a new belief is through a six-step process. Preferably, this is performed first thing in the morning, or right before falling asleep, when the subconscious mind seems to be more impressionable. This increased impressionability may be due to less interference by the conscious mind at these times.

The six steps to building new beliefs are as follows:
I call these the "Six to Fix":

1. Repetition (thought and incantation)

2. Emotion

3. Validation

4. Visualization

5. Work

6. Prayer

Repetition: You need to think of the belief when you first get up in the morning and right before you fall asleep. You can also verbalize by performing incantations.

Emotion: When you are performing your repetitions, you need to feel the joy and peace that comes with already holding the belief.

Validation: This step will be performed sometimes in the morning, and also at random times. This is where you will look for proof in your history and environment, or the history of others, that backs up this belief.

Visualization: You must visualize yourself living the belief and everything it encompasses. The more detail in your visualization, the better.

Work: This is where you educate yourself on anything associated with the belief. There may be action involved here.

Prayer: Last, but definitely not least! Ask God to implant the belief you need, and then accept it as done.

Let us do an example together that may not be too common, and is specific, so you can better see how this works. Your initial beliefs may need to be geared around confidence, communication, negotiation, wisdom, health, etc.

Here is a specific Six to Fix, that I did with my wife. She has always loved horses, but there is a big difference in loving them and training them. She wanted to provide people with a "luxury" trail horse that they could bond with and enjoy. To make this dream a reality, she had to become a great horse trainer, specific to her goals. She had no worries in training our personal horses, but training horses to perform for someone else was a different ball game. As she was contemplating doing this, she knew she must be confident. So, we implemented the Six to Fix.

Repetition: We developed the incantations of:

1. All I need;
   God placed in me!

2. I can do anything;
   My dreams will come true.

3. A well-trained horse;
   Can do any course.

4. A horse with a leader;
   Is better than a feeder.

Emotion: As she would say these, she would focus the majestic feeling of being with a horse. She would feel the joy and confidence that a well-trained horse brings.

Validation: This process involved her looking for signs that as a horse becomes trained, it becomes more connected and happier. She would observe the horses of high-level trainers and see the

CHAPTER 4: BELIEFS

connection that was there, and how much safer the horse was for itself and the rider. She wrote down training successes that she had previously, that proved she could do it.

Visualization: First thing in the morning, and right before bed she would visualize an entire training session from A-Z. She would see herself encountering problems and working through and solving them. She visualized herself handing horses off to happy, new owners. She visualized herself reading letters from customers, exclaiming what a great horse she had connected them with.

Work: This is where we sought out some of the best trainers in the world and did private lessons, seminars, and group trainings. She bought DVDs and books and spent countless hours being around and working with horses. She set a goal to work with at least two horses, six days per week.

Prayer: She had quiet time with God asking for guidance and wisdom. She prayed for a unique connection with these beautiful animals that she respects so much.

So now that you see how to build beliefs, you need a process by which to start looking and building the beliefs you will need to be successful. After using and teaching these techniques to others for many years, I created a belief chart to help sort through this complex subject:

1. Identify your current beliefs in the five priority areas that we will be addressing in Chapter Five (Spiritual, Health, Financial, Character, Relationships).

2. Categorize them in one of two columns: Serving or Nonserving.

3. Rank them in the order you think they will impact your success (Alphabetically, with A being the most important).

4. Rate the belief one to ten; with ten representing 91 to 100 percent conviction, and one representing a very weak belief of 0 to 10 percent conviction.

5. Make an interruption and belief-conditioning plan, beginning with your highest priority beliefs first. If the belief is in the serving column, but it is weak, then it will need more conditioning time. If the belief is in the serving column and it is strong, then it can get less attention. The opposite is true for nonserving beliefs. If a belief is in the nonserving column and it is weak, then it can get less attention; but if it is strong, then it will need more attention to interrupt it. Always start with your nonserving beliefs and then proceed to your serving beliefs.

Let me clarify this a little further. Just like a muscle, all serving beliefs need to be worked out. If you are totally committed to a serving belief, then it will not need a lot of your attention, but it does need to be worked out occasionally. Just remember the analogy of serving beliefs being like muscles. The weaker the muscle and the more important the muscle; the more it needs to be worked out.

In contrast, think of nonserving beliefs like a bad diet. The greater addiction you have to the unhealthy food, the more attention will be needed to interrupt that pattern, and to

CHAPTER 4: BELIEFS

recondition to a choice that serves you better. The takeaway is that all nonserving beliefs must be interrupted and changed.

Here is an analogy: A diesel mechanic does not usually go to a gym to work on his grip strength, because that is something that he uses often, and it is already strong. However, he may go to the gym to stretch his legs and strengthen his low back, because those muscles are probably not worked throughout a full range of motion in his job, making them an area of vulnerability.

Play 4
BELIEFS

1. Create your belief chart, categorizing your Serving and Nonserving beliefs.

Alphabetically rank the beliefs in order of importance.

Rate each belief as to your level of conviction with one being only slightly committed and ten being totally committed, as described in the chapter.

2. Develop a detailed plan based on your chart. The plan should include building, changing, and maintaining beliefs as appropriate. Implement the "Six to Fix" for any beliefs that need to be changed.

  a. Develop incantations to support your new success beliefs and maintenance beliefs. Be sure to repeat them with emotion and motion!

  b. Begin to act as if you already own the new success belief.

  c. Be sure that your mind-movie you created in the last chapter reflects you living out the successful beliefs you have identified.

CHAPTER 5
CLARITY

PROVERBS 29:18: *Where there is no vision, the people perish.*

PSALMS 57:2: *I cry out to God Most High, to God who fulfills his purpose for me.*

JEREMIAH 29:11: *"For I know the plans I have for you," declares the Lord, "plans to prosper you and not to harm you, plans to give you hope and a future."*

---

*"There is nothing more pathetic than
a man with sight but no vision."*
—HELEN KELLER, AUTHOR, BORN BLIND AND DEAF

First, you must get crystal clear on three things:

1. You must be clear on your purpose.

2. You must be clear on who you want to become.

3. You must be clear on exactly what it is you want in five key priority areas. (Health, Relationships, Spiritual, Financial, and Character.)

HABAKKUK 2:2: *Then the Lord replied and said "Write the vision, and make it plain on tablets, so whoever reads it may run with it."*

This scripture teaches us how to start a successful vision. It teaches us to write our vision and to keep it clear and simple. It also teaches us that there must be an action, by stating "so that whoever reads it can run with it."

Here is an example of how being clear is vitally important: If I called you on the phone and said, "Meet me at the mall" and then hung up the phone, the chances of us meeting are slim to none, right? You would probably call me back to ask which mall, and if I said, "Hanes Mall in Winston-Salem," and hung up, our chance of meeting is a little better, but still way off. I am sure you would call again and say, "Listen don't hang up this time, I need to know what day you want to meet, where exactly in the mall, and at what time?"

Now, once I have answered those questions, our chance of meeting would greatly improve. If you asked what I would be

CHAPTER 5: CLARITY

wearing, and asked me to stand by the door, the chances continue to improve. I think you can see that the clearer you are on what you want and why you want it, the greater the chance of you getting it. I am sure you already use this principle in some aspects of your life, but you may not be applying it to the success drivers in your life.

This is so important; I am going to provide one more example. Let us consider the game of golf. Could you imagine if there were no fairways, no greens, and no flag to notate the hole? See, the tee is where you start, or where you are at right now. The fairways are the boundaries you have set to keep yourself on track. The green shows you the direction that you need to continually be shooting for, and the hole shows you exactly where you want to be. There is almost no question that with this level of clarity and direction, everyone will eventually reach the hole. More experienced folks may reach the hole faster, while the less experienced may take much longer, but that is irrelevant; you just have to reach the hole! Let us look at the three areas individually.

PURPOSE:

You are unique. In fact, there is no one else like you anywhere on the planet. Why do you suppose this is? Could it be that you have a Divine purpose? Could it be a purpose that only you are meant to fill? I think it is. Now all you must do is find it. It is okay if you do not know right now, as you start this journey. Just knowing that you need to be clear on your purpose will do for the moment. There are several requirements that must be met to establish your purpose:

1. It must be in line with God's Word.

2. It must serve the greater good.

3. It must be based in love.

4. It must stir your soul and create passion within.

5. It must be propped up with skill. (Remember, skills can always be acquired.)

Without discovering God's purpose for your life, you can never be content. I have found that there are three major things that govern purpose discovery:

1. You must be saved and born again. You cannot discover God's purpose with a human mind. It simply cannot be done. Your true purpose can only be revealed by your Divine Mind. You will learn more about this Divine Mind, but for now just know it is a combination of the Holy Spirit, the subconscious and the supraconscious mind.

2. The more time you spend in God's word, the more He will reveal to you.

3. The more time you spend in total quiet, the more you tap into the power of your Divine Mind.

CHAPTER 5: CLARITY

BECOMING YOU

JOHN 14:20: *When I am raised to life again, you will know that I am in my Father, and you are in me and I am in you.*

You must be clear on who you want to become. You need not know how you will do it, as the process of attainment will yield that. There is no limit to who or what you can become. Answering the following questions will help you establish who it is you want to be:

1. How spiritual do you want to be remembered as being?
   a. Will you be remembered for words, for deeds, or both?

2. What kind of person do you want to be remembered for being, regarding relationships?
   a. Family
   b. Friends
   c. Colleagues
   d. Subordinates
   e. Acquaintances
   f. Strangers

3. How financially well off do you want to be?
   a. At the top (Very wealthy; the sky is the limit)
   b. Above average (Wealthy; you can do most of what you want)
   c. Average (Can get by, but have no risk tolerance)
   d. Below average (Daily struggle)

4. What kind of character traits do you want to be remembered as having?
    a. Did you always lift others or anchor them?
    b. Did you brighten the day or darken it?
    c. Were you always positive or always negative?
    d. Were you a problem solver or a problem creator?
    e. Were you energetic or drab?
    f. Did you seize the day or just exist in it?
    g. Were you known for integrity, or for deceit and corruption?
    h. Was your word your bond or your breach?
    i. Did you present cheer or gloom?
    j. Were you a go-getter or doomed with permanent potential?
    k. Did you foster love or hate?

5. What kind of health did you have spiritually, mentally, and physically?
    a. Were you in great shape with all?
    b. Were you in great shape with one, but not others?
    c. Did you have great spiritual relationships?
    d. Did you eat healthy food choices?
    e. Did you eat mostly junk food?
    f. Did you eat too often and for the wrong reasons?
    g. Did you exercise regularly?
    h. Were you sedentary?
    i. Did you live with vitality or torpidity?

CHAPTER 5: CLARITY

YOUR WANTS

> **MATTHEW 18:3:** *Jesus said, "Truly I tell you, unless you change and become like little children, you will never enter the kingdom of heaven."*

What do you want? Let us consider your wants in five key priority areas: Health, Relationships (with yourself and others), Spiritual, Financial, and Character. Dream BIG, because big dreams yield big actions; likewise, small dreams yield small actions. Think like a child and write down everything you want.

Children do not doubt and question things in the way that adults do. They just believe, and I am asking you to do the same here. Do not worry about or even consider how you will get these things; just write down what you want in a clear and concise fashion. If you are walking with God and living his will, then He desires for you to be prosperous, successful, and to live in abundance. He tells us as much in the scriptures. Let us revisit this scripture again:

> **JEREMIAH 29:11:** *"For I know the plans I have for you," declares the Lord, "plans to prosper you and not to harm you, plans to give you hope and a future."*

Answering the questions under the "becoming you" section will aid with this section as well. The reason is because to get the things you want in each area, you will have to become a person worthy of them. You cannot separate who you are from what you want, because they are one. You can have anything you want if you follow the divine order taught in scripture.

Play 5
CLARITY

1. Clearly define and write your purpose. Your mission statement, so to speak.

   Example: I, Kevin Pyles, will spread God's message of happiness and prosperity to my family and Christians around the world through books, seminars, and deeds, while loving and living the life I teach, and always living in awe.

2. Write your accolade document. You can think of this as being your eulogy in advance. Answer questions like the ones in the "becoming you" section and add things you may want to address. Be sure to start this section with the words, "I am" and not "I will be."

   It is important that you believe and act as if you already are these things.

3. Write down exactly what you want in five key priority areas of Spiritual, Health, Relationships, Financial, and Character. Be sure, in the Relationships section, that you include your relationship with yourself as well as with others. These wants will be made specific in our goals chapter.

   (Remember to think big and include everything you can think of).

CHAPTER 5: CLARITY

EXAMPLES:

I want:

Spiritual
- to draw close to God and understand His will for my life

Health
- to have a normal BMI for my age and height
- to be full of energy every day

Financial
- $5 million in savings
- a vacation home at the beach or mountains

Character
- to be able to effectively communicate with anyone I speak with
- to develop the qualities of success
- to have a library with at least 250 success-related books

Relationships
- to love everything about myself
- a loving, respectful, and supportive spouse
- a family that knows they are my priority
- three to five devoted friends that I can really trust and count on

CHAPTER 6
LEVERAGE

MATTHEW 6:33: *But seek ye first the kingdom of God and his righteousness; and all these things shall be added to you.*

1 CORINTHIANS 7:7: *But every man hath his proper gift of God, one after this manner, and another after that.*

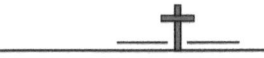

"*Leverage always exists; it is either in your favor or not; nothing in success is neutral.*"
—KEVIN PYLES

> *"Give me a lever long enough and a fulcrum on which to place it, and I shall move the world."*
> —Archimedes, a Greek mathematician

> *"Leverage is the reason some people become rich and others do not become rich."*
> —Robert Kiyosaki

Now that you are clear on exactly what it is that you want, it is imperative that you identify why you want it. This "why" is your leverage, or reasons that you will do what you must do to get those things! The more leverage or reasons you have for each item, the better the chances of you getting it. I always told my fighters that just wanting a trophy would not get them off the stool at the end of round two, when they were beat up and tired. They needed more powerful reasons, like I want to leave a legacy for my son or daughter, or I want to be remembered as one of the best in the world.

We have a saying in the fight world that lends itself to the business world as well, and that is: Fatigue makes cowards of us all. I have seen many brave fighters want to give up when they are exhausted. This happens in life too. Your reasons to succeed must be strong enough to break through the barriers you will inevitably face along the way. Remember that it is not important at this point to know how you will get the things you want, just "why" you must do it—and I do mean "must"!

Leverage is vitally important to the overall success process, so please spend some time here. Trust me, there will be many times along your pathway to success that you will become

CHAPTER 6: LEVERAGE

frustrated, weary, and worried, but do not lose faith; just stick to the process and it will see you through. You must remember that every successful person goes through this, too, and if they say they do not, they are lying. Success is hard, but so is failure! They say hell is dying and meeting the person God meant you to be. The problem with weariness and worry is that they magnify your obstacles, making them appear much bigger than they really are. If you already accept this up front and know that it will happen, you can "beef up" your leverage on the front end to handle anything that comes your way thereafter. I once heard an Olympic wrestler say that he would always tell himself that he wanted to face the absolute toughest competitors out there. By doing this, he was never nervous when he saw the brackets and realized he had a tough competitor in it. He had already established in his mind that he only wanted the best, so there was nothing to get nervous about.

Here is an example of how wants and leverage work:

I place a two-inch-thick by six-inch-wide by ten-foot-long (2 x 6 x 10) board on cinder blocks approximately one foot in the air. At the end of the board, I put a $100 bill. All you must do is walk across the board and you get the 100 dollars. You want to cross the board because you want the money. You think of what all you would do with the money and what the chances of you falling and getting hurt would be. Since the board is only one foot in the air, you do not associate much risk versus the reward.

Now if we take that same board and put it twenty feet in the air, your obstacle just became much bigger. You would look much harder at this situation. You would probably equate the chance of falling and injuring yourself to be greater than that of getting 100 dollars, and would probably decide it's just not worth it.

However, if we improve the reasons for crossing the higher board or, in other words, get more leverage, you may still be willing to cross. What if I said that the new reward for crossing is that I would pay off your home, automobiles, and all other debt, and give you $5,000 a week for life? Your reasons, or leverage, for crossing just got a lot bigger. Now you would most likely be willing to risk the fall because you have given yourself enough leverage. The bigger the perceived risk, the more leverage you will need.

I think you can now see how leverage works, so come up with as many reasons as possible that you absolutely must achieve your dreams. It is impossible to foresee all the obstacles you will encounter. Your symbolic board to cross will continually be raised and lowered along the way without your control but the one thing you can control is your reasons for crossing.

CHAPTER 6: LEVERAGE

Play 6

LEVERAGE

1. Write down all the reasons that you absolutely must achieve the dreams that you wrote down in Play 5. Remember, the more reasons you have, the better!

CHAPTER 7
GOALS

PROVERBS 16:3: *Commit thy works unto the Lord, and thy thoughts shall be established.*

Based on this scripture, I developed this acronym:

Goals are:

Godly
Objectives
Assuring
Lasting
Success

"Goals are simply dreams with deadlines."
—Napoleon Hill, motivational speaker
and self-help writer

"Goals are your dreams in work clothes."
—Dave Ramsey, businessman, author,
and motivational speaker

These are wise statements, because they give you the visual that there will have to be some effort put forth. Out of the hundreds of books, tapes, and programs I have studied, I cannot remember any that did not contain goal setting. Probably everyone you talk to mentions something about a goal they have or have had at some point. Granted, they may not have the "goal setting/goal obtaining" knowledge, but they have goals just the same. So, the question then becomes: If goal setting is such common knowledge, then why aren't more people achieving them?

I believe there are two main reasons that goals are not achieved. First, the goal is not composed properly; secondly, as we talked about with beliefs, the goal is set in the conscious mind, while much of the achievement needs to occur in the subconscious mind. The latter means—to return to our earlier metaphor from computer science—that the formula is typed on the screen, but there are no programs installed running in the background to complete the daily task necessary to reach the goal. Your true beliefs and habits must be in perfect harmony with your conscious goals to obtain the desired result. Once you establish your goals, you will want to go back and visit the chapters on habits and beliefs, to ensure that they

CHAPTER 7: GOALS

are in line with your goals. Goals are the first step in making the invisible, visible. They are a means by which we create the future in advance.

Many personal development speakers have referenced the "Harvard study of 1979" or "Yale study of 1953," although there is much debate to whether it actual happened. I do not believe it took place, but it does not really matter if it happened or not, if you believe that the outcome would have happened as they say it did. In a nutshell, the study proposed that the graduating MBA class was asked, "Have you set clear written goals for your future, and have you made plans to accomplish them?" The results of that question were that only 3 percent had written goals and plans; *13* percent had goals, but not in writing; and 84 percent had no specific goals at all. Upon following up with this same group ten years later, Harvard interviewed the members of that class again and found that the 13 percent who had goals but not in writing were earning on average twice as much as the 84 percent of those who had no goals at all; while the 3 percent who had clear, written goals were earning on average 10 times as much as the other 97 percent of graduates altogether. The only difference between the groups was having clear, written goals.

You must admit it makes for an exceptional story on the justification of written goals. True or not, I believe it to be sound advice. The first step of good goal writing is to know how to create one.

Every goal MUST have 11 parts:

1. Must be Godly

2. Must be prayed over

3. Must be written

4. Must be specific

5. Must be measurable

6. Must be timed

7. Must be owned

8. Must be cross-referenced with obstacles

9. Must be broken into actions

10. Must be visualized as already achieved

11. Must be reviewed and scored daily

I have mentored many people over the years, and some of them had great goals in their head, but that is where they stayed. I found that the reasons for this generally fall into one or more of five categories:

1. Fear: Afraid of failure or success

2. Knowledge: Have goals, but not formed correctly

3. Motivation: Lack the drive to sit down and do it

CHAPTER 7: GOALS

4. Arrogance: Do not think they need to write their goals

5. Ignorance: Never heard or learned about goal setting

I think everyone can acknowledge how easy it is to get "caught up" in the business of daily life. If your goals are not written down and referenced, then trivial things pop up throughout the day that push your goals further and further down the priority list and out of your mind. By looking at a goal, you are refocusing on what you have established as important, and you are impressing it on your subconscious mind. Without a written "map" of what is important many people will start self-gratifying—that is, doing whatever feels the best now rather than what is best for the long-term.

Most achievers will trade temporary comfort for long-term gain. Do not get me wrong; this must be done in balance, by enjoying the now and not just always preparing for a future that you keep pushing further down the road!

> *"Man is born to live and not to prepare to live."*
> —BORIS PASTERNAK, RUSSIAN POET

I think you need a balance of both. I once heard someone say that you must stop and smell the roses, just don't pitch a tent! Many things that seem like a sacrifice in the beginning will become pleasurable to you as you see yourself moving toward your dreams. There is no better character builder than all the stuff that must be done to obtain an 11-part goal. It is not the writing of the goal, but the changes that you will have to make in yourself to reach the goal, that builds the character.

"Glory lies in the attempt to reach one's goal, not in reaching it."
—Mahatma Gandhi

Let us look at a sample goal that one of my fitness salesman set:

Area: Finance

Godly: I want to help people change their lifestyles to become their best version of themselves.

Prayer: Lord, I know that our bodies are your temple here on Earth. I ask for the wisdom, energy, and perseverance to reach as many people as possible to guide them into health and vitality. Please allow me to use the right words and set the right example to let them see You, through me. Amen.

Primary Goal: I will increase my salary by $20,000 within 12 months which will be December 31, 20xx.

Obstacles: 1. I have only been in sales for one year and lack education and experience. 2. I do not have polished communication skills. 3. I do not currently have enough prospects.

ACTION GOALS:

1. I will spend one hour per day, from 8:00 a.m. to 9:00 a.m., in sales education, consisting of books, seminars, and videos.

2. I will generate at least ten new leads per day through social media and cold calls from 11:00 a.m. to 1:00 p.m., and I will obtain one referral from each new client.

3. I will maintain a weekly appointment closing ratio of 52 percent, which I will calculate every Friday at 4:00 p.m.

Visualization: The salesman took 5 minutes and visualized himself telling his spouse that he now makes $20,000 per year more. He visualized himself making many positive phone calls. He visualized how he would feel inside, the increased pride and peace that would come with the extra income.

(Here we have 10 of the 11 parts: Godly, prayed, written, specific, measurable, timed, owned-he wrote it for himself, cross-referenced with obstacles, broken into action goals, visualized.)

(Number 11, reviewed and scored daily, will be achieved from this day forward and recorded on his daily CHAMP scorecard, which I will explain shortly.)

You will want to set your goals in five primary areas. (Finance/Relationship/Health/Spiritual/Character) Generally, I recommend only focusing on three areas at a time. This is important to stay balanced in your life.

Play 7
GOALS

1. Write down the five focus areas:
   a. Spiritual
   b. Finance
   c. Relationship
   d. Health
   e. Character

2. Beside each area put a happiness factor from zero to ten. Zero being totally unsatisfied in the area to ten being totally satisfied in the area. This will allow you to focus on the three areas which are negatively impacting your life the most. Please note, you can select one area that is not necessarily one of the lowest if it is an area that you really want to focus on. I recommend having your spiritual life at an eight out of ten before addressing other areas.

3. Write three primary goals, one in each of the initial three focus areas you selected.

4. Write two or three of the main obstacles that may cause you trouble in attaining the goal. If you cannot think of any, that is okay, they will remind you when they come up.

CHAPTER 7: GOALS

5. Break each primary goal down into two or three action goals.

On the following pages, I have included a sample goal-setting worksheet and a CHAMP Scorecard, to help monitor your progress.

FOCUS AREAS	HAPPINESS FACTOR RATING
Spiritual	8
Health	5
Financial	5
Relationships	6
Character	6

PRIMARY GOAL

1. _____

   a. Obstacle: _____

   b. Obstacle: _____

   c. Obstacle _____

      i. Action Goal: _____

      ii. Action Goal: _____

      iii. Action Goal: _____

THE DIVINE PLAYBOOK

CHAMP SCORECARD

(CHECKOFFS HELP ACHIEVE MY PLAN)

Date: _____ Day: _____

Focus Area: _____

Primary Goal #: _____

Did I do 100% of Action Goal 1? Yes ( ) No ( )
Obstacles noted: Yes ( ) No ( )

If no (why not):

Remedy:

Did I do 100% of Action Goal 2? Yes ( ) No ( )
Obstacles noted: Yes ( ) No ( )

If no (why not):

Remedy:

Did I do 100% of Action Goal 3? Yes ( ) No ( )
Obstacles noted: Yes ( ) No ( )

If no (why not):

CHAPTER 7: GOALS

Remedy:

Focus Area: _____

Primary Goal #: _____

Did I do 100% of Action Goal 1? Yes ( ) No ( )
Obstacles noted: Yes ( ) No ( )

If no (why not):

Remedy:

Did I do 100% of Action Goal 2? Yes ( ) No ( )
Obstacles noted: Yes ( ) No ( )

If no (why not):

Remedy:

Did I do 100% of Action Goal 3? Yes ( ) No ( )
Obstacles noted: Yes ( ) No ( )

If no (why not):

Remedy:

Focus Area: _____

Primary Goal #: _____

Did I do 100% of Action Goal 1? Yes ( ) No ( )
Obstacles noted: Yes ( ) No ( )

If no (why not):

Remedy:

Did I do 100% of Action Goal 2? Yes ( ) No ( )
Obstacles noted: Yes ( ) No ( )

If no (why not):

Remedy:

Did I do 100% of Action Goal 3? Yes ( ) No ( )
Obstacles noted: Yes ( ) No ( )

If no (why not):

Remedy:

CHAPTER 8
GETTING REAL

John 16:33: *These things I have spoke unto you, that in me ye might have peace. In the world ye shall have tribulation: but be of good cheer; I have overcome the world.*

"An ounce of reality will prevent a pound of regret."
—Kevin Pyles

My grandfather used to say that an ounce of prevention is worth a world of cure.

I like that saying, and so I came up with one of my own—the one you just read, above.

One of the most common mistakes I see is that people often do not "get real" with themselves before they begin an endeavor. Vince Lombardi alluded to the fact that when you plan for success, you must be willing to get up and work at your dream every day, while still realizing that, for the moment, you are still exactly where you are.

Another saying that my grandfather passed down to me was that every carpenter expects to smash his finger. What he was trying to teach me is that if you expect things to be tough, then you are not so overwhelmed when things get tough, and you simply keep moving forward. This thought process is extremely beneficial for anyone who is trying to become successful. Research has proven that expecting a realistic and tough course greatly increases the chances that you will stay the course.

I have an analogy that I like to use to make this stick in people's minds. You do not plan to hike Mount Everest in flip-flops. This example seems a little obvious, but it gets right to the point. Just like not planning well to hike Mount Everest will get you killed, not planning well for goal obtainment will kill your dreams.

I saw this principle at play all the time with the mixed martial arts side of my martial arts academy. Here is an example that was quite common: A young man sits at home and watches an MMA fight. He gets excited thinking about the fame and money that comes from being an MMA champion. He sees himself holding that shiny gold belt with thousands of screaming fans, and he thinks to himself, Finally, an easy way to make money. Here is the way it breaks down:

Fighter comes to the gym.

CHAPTER 8: GETTING REAL

Coach: May I help you?

Fighter: I want to be an MMA fighter.

Coach: Great. What is your background?

Fighter: I fight and wrestle with my friends all the time and we know a lot of the moves. I can beat all my friends. We watch all the fights together on TV.

Coach: Okay. So how long have you been thinking about fighting competitively?

Fighter: Off and on for a few months, but after that fight the other night, I knew I wanted to do it.

Coach: Awesome. To see where you are at in your planning, I have a few questions for you.

Fighter: Okay.

Coach: Have you budgeted the cost of training into your personal finances? You will have to pay for training, purchase training gear, and deal with training injuries along the way.

Fighter: I am looking for work now, so it should not be a problem when I find a job.

Coach: Do you have a wife or kids? Because this is very time-consuming, and if you do this, it should probably be a family decision.

Fighter: Yes, I have a wife and a three-year-old son, but she is okay with me doing it.

Coach: How many days a week do you think you will be able to train? Most successful fighters train six days per week, with a minimum of three to five hours per day, and this number increases as you move up in the ranks and into bigger and better events.

Fighter: Wow, that may be hard for me, because I do not have transportation yet.

Coach: Okay, let us do this. We can put you on a one-month trial to see how all of this works out, and then you can make better decisions from there.

Fighter: Okay.

Coach: Go ahead and change, and you can get with the guys. They are getting ready to start a dynamic warm-up routine that should take about thirty minutes.

Fighter: Okay.

Coach: Now that you are warmed up, you can start learning and drilling technique for the next couple of hours.

At the end of the night.

Fighter: Boy, I did not realize how out of shape I was. I have not really been doing anything and I am totally exhausted. That was much harder than I expected.

Coach: I know, and this is just the beginning. I need you to start jogging three to five miles every morning, with sprint intervals, and we need to get you with the dietitian, who will help you with learning what to eat. You also need to stay hydrated and get at least eight to ten hours of sleep each night to allow your body to recover.

Fighter: I just do not think I am ready for this right now. I probably will come back in a few months.

Coach: I understand. Professional fighting is an extremely tough career choice. Go home and think about it,

CHAPTER 8: GETTING REAL

and if you still want to do it, start working on a plan. You need to address the things we spoke about. We are happy to help you achieve your goal of fighting in any way we can.

You can see how it is quite easy to focus on the dream without the obstacles. Please do not misunderstand here; I am 100 percent in favor of setting difficult goals. However, it is imperative that you identify as many obstacles as possible and prepare for them as best you can. I like to look at it this way. The more setbacks you have along the way to your dreams, the more you have accomplished once you get there. During the years I spent running our MMA team, I literally watched boys transform into men and girls into women. Not because of the fighting itself, but because the discipline it took to succeed in the fight world transferred to all aspects of their life. These young fighters learn several valuable lessons: That they cannot make it alone, they must identify their strengths and weaknesses, and they must, above all, have a daily discipline in their approach.

I have a motto: "A goal that is set in reality never changes; even though the approach may often change." I always tell young people that achieving a goal will not be as important as the man or woman they will have to become to attain it.

Play 8
GETTING REAL

1. Write a brief paragraph of exactly where you are right now in your life and how you will work every day toward your dreams, all while realizing that, for a while, you will still be right where you are.

2. Make a list of your weaknesses, and beside each one, plan for how you will address it. Doing this will prevent them from surprising you down the road.

3. Make a list of your strengths and how you will capitalize on those strengths to set you up for success.

4. Review and rethink your obstacles that you addressed in your goal-setting session. Ask someone with experience if they can think of anything that you may be missing.

5. Take a moment to pray for perseverance. Through your weakness shines God's strength.

CHAPTER 9
FOCUS

PROVERBS 4:25: *Let your eyes look straight ahead; fix your gaze before you.*

PHILIPPIANS 4:8: *Finally, brethren, whatsoever things are true, whatsoever things are honest, whatsoever things are just, whatsoever things are pure, whatsoever things are lovely, whatsoever things are of good report; if there be any virtue, and if there be any praise; think on these things.*

In Proverbs chapter 23, verse 7, it says: For as he thinketh in his heart, so is he. What you think about and honestly believe, you will become. All focused thought that is backed by 100

percent belief must manifest itself externally. That is the law of creation. There is no doubt in my mind that you always find what you are looking for.

Said differently: "Where you focus, you will find." Negative people always find the negative in every situation; likewise, positive people find the positive in every situation. My favorite analogy for this is the "new car" analogy, because almost everyone I have talked to has experienced it. Let us say you wanted to buy a new Jeep, so you started researching and thinking about Jeeps. You were thinking about color, tires, model, and all that fun stuff. After you have decided that you want a candy-apple red Jeep, it seems like you are seeing candy-apple red Jeeps everywhere you go. You see them on the highway, at the store, and everywhere in between.

Has this happened to you? Do you think that once you decided to buy a red Jeep that everyone hurried out, bought one, and started driving near you? Of course not. The shiny red Jeeps were always there, but your subconscious did not believe red Jeeps to be important to you, so it did not pick them out of your environment. Opportunity works in the same way. If you program your mind with a clear focus on what is important to you, then it will always be scanning your environment to find things that match up. The remarkable thing is that once you have programmed a clear focus on what is important, you do not have to work near as hard to find it.

Many people often confuse this with luck. Have you heard someone say, "That guy is so lucky; he always gets the great opportunities"? Maybe it was not luck at all. Maybe that guy knows how to set a clear vision. A vision which allows him to

CHAPTER 9: FOCUS

see any opportunity that crosses his path, so rather than missing out, he capitalizes on them.

I want you to think of your brain like it is a new, eight-week-old puppy. In the beginning, it is difficult to get the puppy to do anything except run amok and react to the environment. If you put him on a leash, he will pull right, left, backward, many combinations of those. That puppy is in pure self-gratification mode; a sniff here, a kibble of food there, a cricket here . . . you get the point. It will be nearly impossible to walk him down a straight line to get from one place to another. Now, if you do not spend any time training that puppy with clear direction, what do you think will happen? It will grow up into a dog that is just as rambunctious and extremely hard to control. On the other hand, an expertly trained puppy becomes a dog that will not even put pressure on the leash when you walk him. He keeps his head up, shoulder by your leg, and awaits his next cue.

I believe the human brain is much like that new puppy. It will always naturally want to pull you toward immediate self-gratification. It is your job to train your brain how to focus on what is important and what must be done daily to get you where you need to be in the most efficient way possible. You will be amazed at how many more opportunities and possibilities present themselves when your subconscious mind knows what to focus on. You will pick opportunities out of thin air that never seemed to be there before, just like that red Jeep! Once your subconscious mind accepts the belief that you will succeed no matter what and it knows what to focus on, it will work tirelessly, 24/7 on bringing it to fruition.

One of the best ways to stay focused on the "big picture" is using a vision board. This is a board where you put pictures that directly reflect what it is you want to accomplish. The pictures need not only be material items like a dream house or a boat, but also can be of health, happiness, or anything else your heart desires. I prefer clear, vibrant pictures with as much detail as possible. I recommend having a main vision board at home and then smaller ones for work, in your vehicle or anywhere else that you spend time on a regular basis. With the modern technology of today, you can take a picture of your vision board with your phone and then set reminders to pop up at certain times of the day, reminding you to look at the board and visualize those accomplishments. When you do this, you are deeply imprinting your subconscious mind with what to focus on. Your brain responds well to pictures, so this is one of the best ways to train it. To me, vision boards are the fun part of the playbook. You get to see your future in advance, and you conjure up all the feelings that are associated with accomplishing your dreams.

I would say that the lack of focus, only behind confidence, probably robs more people of success and happiness than most other things combined. When I refer to focus, remember, I am referring to clear focus, down to the smallest detail. For example, if I am going to have an important conversation, I always focus on the desired result. I define in advance what I would like the outcome of the interaction to be, so my subconscious has a clear focus on what I need for the interaction to be a success. If I am coming home from work to see my wife and kids, then I will focus on exactly how I would like each one of them to feel. I do this before I get there, so my subconscious will bring forth all

CHAPTER 9: FOCUS

the wisdom I need to accomplish the task. I believe that if you do not do these things, then you simply become a by-product of the environment or situation which could sometimes work out, but in most cases, will not. In short, you either create the situation or become a by-product of it.

It is imperative that you learn to focus on positive, supportive thoughts. Most people tend to have numerous negative thoughts. I, myself, used to have more negative thoughts than positive ones; perhaps this rings true with you. When you have a thought that reflects an unsupportive emotion like fear, anxiety, angry, sad, etc. . . . then you know that you are out of sync with the way God created you to be, because in Galatians chapter 5, verse 22, it states: "But the fruit of the Spirit is love, joy, peace, longsuffering, gentleness, goodness, faith, meekness, temperance." If you are having thoughts and emotions not of the Spirit, then you are greatly hindering the "Divine Mind" from manifesting your destiny. You need not be able to think of an entire solution to a given problem, but you must flip any negative thought to a positive one.

To train my mind to rid itself of negative thoughts, I developed a strategy which I call "flipping." Here is how flipping works: When you have a negative thought, you should immediately flip it to a positive thought. Remember, I am a lifelong martial artist, so I had to have some fun with this. When I have a negative thought or emotion, I picture the thought as a cartoon guy in a martial-arts uniform, and immediately my cartoon Judoka (a person who practices the art of Judo, which excels in throwing) runs in, gets his grip on the negative thought, and flips it to a positive one. This cartoon Judoka is the "gatekeeper" of my mind.

My gatekeeper protects my destiny by not allowing negative thoughts to get through.

I once had an employee notice that I did this regularly. She asked, "How do you always manage to make something negative into something positive?" I explained to her that the situation was there whether I viewed it as positive or negative, so I choose to see it in a way that benefits me, instead of a way that robs me of my destiny. I did not tell her about my cartoon Judoka, because without knowing the entire process I thought she may have me committed. This is an immensely powerful practice, and once it becomes a habit you will never be the same.

You should be aware that this can be quite a bit of work initially, because you may have more frequent negative thoughts than you realized. I am sure you have met someone who can somehow see the negative in every situation, haven't you? Hopefully, this person is not in the mirror, but if so, you will overcome this. I know, this concept may seem a little crazy to you, but it is no crazier than having recurring, irrational, negative thoughts that kill your drive and paralyze your abilities to act toward attainment of your dreams. You may be predisposed to negative thinking by nature, but you can rewire your brain and rid yourself of toxic, negative thinking by implementing the "flipping" strategy.

To take this a step further, I use a garden analogy with my kids. I explained to them that that if their Judoka does not flip the negative thought, then that thought is allowed in, and it plants a briar in the garden of their mind. This briar will easily grow and spread to take over their garden and sabotage their dreams. On the flip side (pun intended), if their Judoka flips the negative thought to a positive one, then that positive thought

CHAPTER 9: FOCUS

plants a fruit tree. That fruit tree will also grow, giving fruit to nourish their dreams. Every thought that enters your mind will either be a briar or a fruit tree! Furthermore, if you are not having strategic, positive thoughts, a briar will spread to an empty space, making you more negative. Just like the soil yearns to fill any empty space, so it is with the garden of your mind. Your goal should be to fill all space, by planting as many fruit trees as you can each day, and to block the planting of briars.

I cannot think of anyone who would like a garden full of briars over fruits. Can you? Yet it is more common than not. You must guard your mind with full resolve if you want to reach your dreams. I will warn you here that once you teach your children this, they will be ready to use it against you. As soon as they see you angry or worried, they will say, "Are you growing briars, right now?" Kids often grasp this stuff better than adults, because they do not have as many counter beliefs to get in their way like adults usually do. In other words, adults are much more apt to use a "yes, but" strategy of why something cannot work for them.

Mark Twain once said, "You can't depend on your eyes when your imagination is out of focus." This is so true. As I said earlier, you will always see what your subconscious is focused on. Your daily focus will ultimately become your reality, and your reality will manifest your destiny. Have you ever noticed that if you are focused on a problem, you seem to have more of them? You know, getting smacked down while you are down type of stuff. You are not really having more problems; you are simply more aware of the ones you have. I remember one time, a young fighter said, "Coach, how can I ever get to where you are, so I won't have all of these problems?" To him I seemed like the guy with no problems, but what he did not know was that at that very moment I was dealing with the following:

1. I had a furnace that had just quit on me, which caused a pipe to freeze and bust in a home that I had for sale.

2. I had a roof leak on a business property that was proving to be hard to find.

3. We were going through a remodel at our health club, and it was proving exceedingly difficult to balance spatial and budget needs.

4. The farmhouse that we had just moved into had a water stove that had a busted tank, so we did not have our primary heat source, and it was winter!

5. The one-half-mile driveway to the farmhouse had all but washed out, making it a mud-bogging trip to get in and out of there.

6. I was having meeting after meeting with many of my rehabilitation clients on how to cut the cost of our services, because of the pressures they faced from the downward spiral of the healthcare market at the time.

7. I was going to have to cut positions in the company for the first time ever, in order to provide relief to clients and keep

CHAPTER 9: FOCUS

the company healthy. It is difficult to let people go when they have not done anything wrong except be hired last.

My answer to him was this: "Look, you are never going to be without problems, but what you can be without is a mindset that magnifies them."

I am sure anyone reading this book could list four or five problems they are facing right now. The key is to never focus on the problem but on the small steps that will move you toward the solution.

Here is how I explained my problems to him:

1. Bad furnace/busted pipe: Thank goodness, the pipe was in the garage, so a neighbor saw the water in the driveway and called me. Also, I knew a trusted plumber that I could call right away.

2. Leaky Roof: I was so fortunate to own a commercial building like this at my age, and once the roof was replaced, we would be good for another 20 years.

3. Remodel: We were remodeling because our volumes were growing, and we had figured out what our members were wanting.

4. Water stove: I had always dreamed of owning a farm, and the house had a small backup gas heater and we had fireplaces to help in some rooms, so the kids could stay warm.

5. Driveway: This was a great manual labor project to do with my kids. Kids need manual labor, and this was a great chance to spend quality time while gaining sweat equity in our property.

6. Distraught clients: I was thankful that I had developed good enough relationships where my clients would come to me and ask for help, rather than just ending the relationship at the next opportunity.

7. Cutting positions: Although some people would lose their job, we had much staff that still had good jobs, so I chose to focus on how we have protected their positions, instead of the ones we were losing.

I explained to him that when he sees people who seem to not have problems, what he is really seeing is people who have learned to focus on solutions, thereby projecting success rather than failure.

CHAPTER 9: FOCUS

Play 9
FOCUS

1. Create two or three vision boards that reflect your dreams in the five key focus areas: Finance, Relationship, Health, Spiritual, and Character. Put the boards where you will see them daily. You can also do this on your phone, by either taking a picture of your vision board, or creating an album representative of each of your focus areas and saving pictures into each album accordingly. You can even go a step further and create reminders in your phone that pop up and notify you to look at your vision board.

2. Review the goals you set for yourself daily and measure your success by using the CHAMP scorecard each day.

3. Use incantations throughout the day, especially first thing in the morning and right before bed, to remain focused on the positive.

4. Implement the flipping technique as described in the chapter.

CHAPTER 10
GET DECISIVE

JAMES 1:6: *But let him ask in faith, nothing wavering. For he that wavereth is like a wave of the sea, driven with the wind and tossed.*

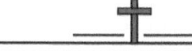

> *"You will become the sum total of the daily decisions you make or don't make."*
> —KEVIN PYLES

There is much more of an art to making decisions than may appear at first blush. Learning how to make decisions is an invaluable skill. I believe that this process has six parts. Great decisions are:

1. Timely
2. Weighed
3. Believed
4. Bounced
5. Turned over
6. Followed by action

Let us discuss each part.

TIMELY

Being timely means that you do not fall victim to the paralysis of analysis. You can analyze something to the point of being afraid to do anything. Which is still a decision, by the way. You need to have a tentative deadline to making every decision.

WEIGHED

A weighed decision is a decision where the consequences have been assessed. The bigger the consequences, the more time allotted to the decision-making process. This does not mean you drag it out and become paralyzed, as we noted about the first principle. It simply means that you allow more time for a decision with bigger consequences.

BELIEVED

Believing in your decisions is imperative. As an entrepreneur, I struggled with this in my early years of business. Entrepreneurs must make many decisions, many of which may be outside of their skill set. Entrepreneurs are often the CEO, CFO, HRO, COO, technician, and sometimes the support staff. I will never

CHAPTER 10: GET DECISIVE

forget the day I was talking to a very accomplished CEO, and he asserted that even the greatest CEOs never know if their decisions are right, they just make them and move forward. This concept changed my life, because I had always assumed that the reason I felt uneasy was because of something I did not know, due to not having attended business school or not having a father that guided me. Things changed instantly for me when I adopted the belief of believing in my decisions and moving forward. Believing in your decisions is more important than making them. Remember, no one has a crystal ball.

BOUNCED

You can bounce your decisions off trusted people. You can always ask the advice of people you respect or people with more experience than you. This can be a good idea as long as you still make the decision yourself and own it!

TURNED OVER

The turnover technique is a great strategy; however, it does require a certain level of mental mastery. I developed this strategy after much study on mental science and the power of the subconscious mind. As a Christian, I refer to this as the "Divine Mind." This is the universal intelligence of the Holy Spirit. This technique is where you turn over a decision to the Divine Mind and then get out of its way. Here is how it works:

1. Go to a quiet place. I prefer this to be somewhere in nature, but it does not have to be. It does need to be a place free from distraction.

2. Propose the question to the Divine Mind and tell it when you need the answer by.

3. You now must believe with 100 percent certainty that the answer will be given to you.

4. Relax for around thirty to sixty minutes just looking at the splendor of nature or just being in a relaxed state. It is important that you not be trying to think on the question or the answer. Just as the name implies, you have turned it over, and it is no longer your concern.

5. When you get a "gut feeling," a hunch, or a strong sense of the answer, then you go with it. Be sure not to second-guess your decision once your conscious mind becomes involved because that often happens. Once you get the answer from your Divine Mind, go with it.

ACTION

Your decisions must be followed by action. Once you have made a decision it is imperative that you take an initial action to solidify it.

STAYING ON TRACK

Here, we will discuss business owners and nonbusiness owners. Being a business owner basically means you are a nonstop problem solver, and if you are not careful, you can become inundated with many mundane tasks throughout the day. Many of the things you deal with could be solved at a lower level, but are often shuffled up to avoid responsibility.

CHAPTER 10: GET DECISIVE

I want you to think of each day like a long hike. You want to keep your backpack as light as possible. Every time someone brings you a problem, I want you to think of it like it is a brick going into your backpack. It will not take long before your backpack is too heavy to carry, and you may still have a long way to go that day. This can happen in your personal life too. There are several reasons people will bring you problems. Some of the reasons are lack of accountability, laziness, ignorance, inexperience, unawareness, trust, and more. After realizing what a huge factor this was in my success plan, I started studying this. After much research, I decided to base my plan on "The Eisenhower Principle."

Eisenhower said, "What is important is seldom urgent, and what is urgent is seldom important." Steven Covey really popularized this theory in his book, *The 7 Habits of Highly Effective People*, when he displayed a decision-making matrix consisting of four quadrants. Covey put it like this:

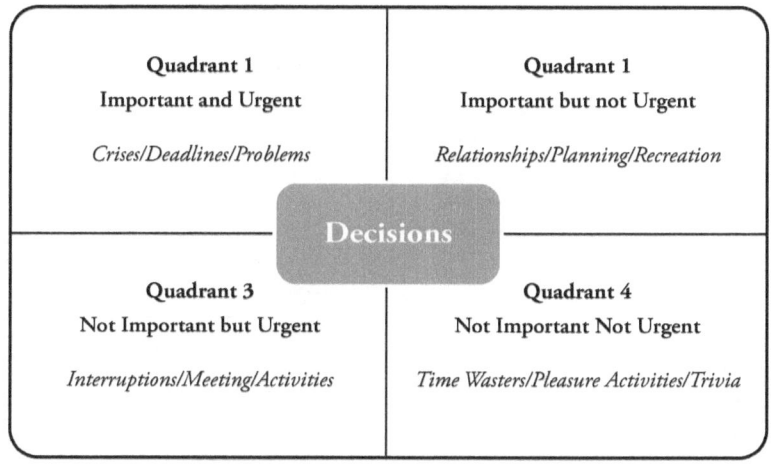

As you start dealing with more and more people, it does not take long to learn that the blacker and whiter you can make things, with no shades of gray, the smoother things will run. The more time you spend on processes on the front end, the more organized, efficient, and enjoyable it will be on the back end. I used the Eisenhower principle in two ways, a standard version for my own decisions and an expanded version that I created for my subordinates. I created a variation of the matrix by adding a solution process. Here is the one I created:

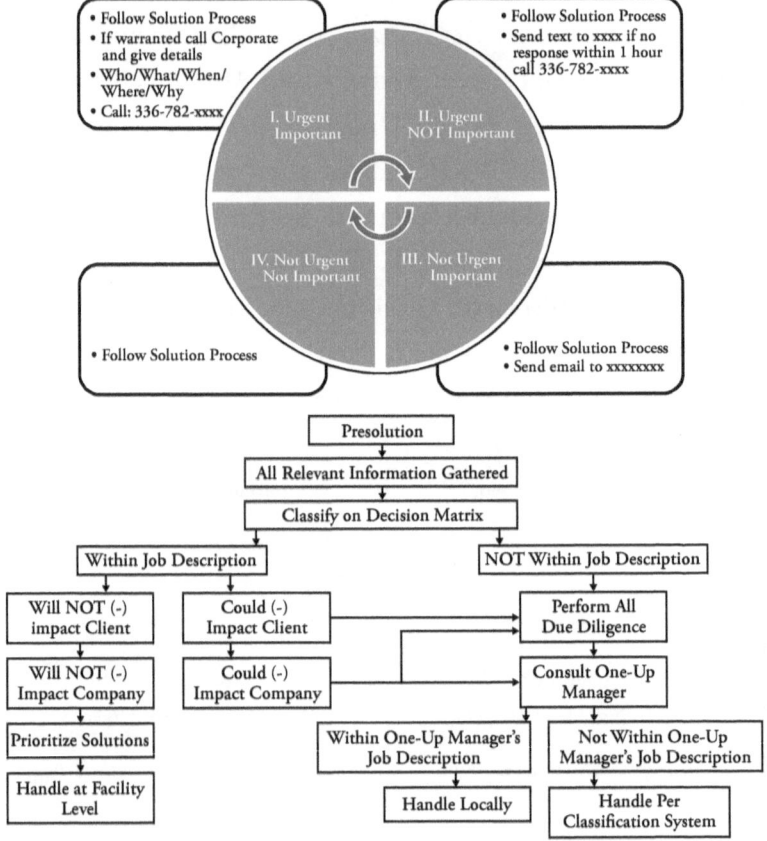

I realize this may seem tedious, but believe me, this greatly enhanced my time savings and allowed me to stay focused on

CHAPTER 10: GET DECISIVE

my priority items. Anthony Robbins once said, "People who are happy and successful are simply asking better questions." My question was, "How can I run this company while staying focused on the things I need to make it a success?"

Another good strategy to maintain your day is the If /Then strategy. Hundreds of research studies have proven that an "If/Then" strategy is much more effective than just randomly saying you will do something. "If/Then "strategies work like this: If it is 2:00 p.m., then I will make thirty prospecting calls. If it is 6:00 a.m., then I will jog for 30 minutes. If it is 5:30 pm then I will leave the office and head home.

This is a fitting example of being decisive, and why I like this strategy so much. It removes the possibility of changing your schedule and getting caught up with things that are not supportive to your goals and dreams. This is the way decisions were intended to be made. Decide is derived from the Latin word "decidare." De means "off" and cidare means "to cut." Said differently, it means that once you decide something that is important, you do not go back on it, you simply do it! You have cut off from all other options. Burned the ship, so to speak.

I know this is easier said than done, but that is where all these principles start tying together. You must develop a belief system on decision-making in which once you decide something, then that is it. This gets easier to do as you become proficient at making better decisions. If you are not sure where to start on a decision, then sometimes it is good to imagine what you think someone you trust would tell you. Just pretend that they are giving you advice and see what direction that takes you. As odd as it may seem, this will sometimes trigger an answer that had evaded you before.

One last strategy that you can utilize is to read biographies of people that you admire and respect. This allows you to develop a thorough knowledge of their personality and character traits. With this information, you can develop an imaginary council of great minds. This is a council where you can pose a pressing question to each one of them and then think or feel as to how they would respond. This could fall under the "bounced" part of the decision process. It is particularly important to be in a quiet and calm space, such as with the turnover technique, to allow for a good flow of energy. I have been helped by this before, and it is a neat strategy; just be sure no one hears you talking to your imaginary council because you may get committed before you reach your dreams!

A final thought on decisions is to never make important ones under either of the two following conditions:

1. If you are under the influence of alcohol, prescription drugs, or similar

2. If you are in a highly emotional state, whether those emotions be extremely positive or extremely negative.
    a. If I am highly emotional, I always step back and distance myself from a decision.
    b. I will circle back around to it when I am in a more neutral state of mind.

Please do not confuse this with procrastination. I always set deadlines on decisions; however, I always factor in my current state of mind before making them.

CHAPTER 10: GET DECISIVE

Play 10
GETTING DECISIVE

1. Design a decision-making tree for yourself and any people who directly report to you. Develop the action steps and timelines that should be followed. The clearer and more concise it is, the better it will work for you. Be sure to teach it to anyone who should be using it. Remember to be black-and-white, with no shades of gray.

2. For the next four weeks, start a decision-making journal. This should be a separate notebook that has only questions and decisions in it. Start logging the questions, and under each question include the six parts:
   a. Timely—Set a deadline.
   b. Weighed—Rate it from one to ten, with ten being extremely important due to larger consequences.
   c. Believed in—Do not second-guess yourself. Write down several reasons that gave you the leverage to decide as you did.
   d. Bounced—If needed, seek wise counsel and record it here.
   e. Turned over—This is an important step, because your Divine Mind will always steer you in the right direction 6. Followed by action—List the action(s) taken after the decision was made.

3. Review. At the end of four weeks review your journal, and see if you can find any patterns or improvements.

4. Be sure that you are making the decisions and not allowing others to make them for you. You can seek guidance, but you must make the call. After four weeks, you should be able to do this without the journal. You will continue to become quicker and more efficient with practice.

CHAPTER 11
ACTION

PROVERBS 24:27: *Prepare thy work without and make it fit for thyself in the field; afterwards build thine house.*

JAMES 2:14: *What good is it, my brothers, if someone says he has faith but does not have works? Can such faith save them?*

JAMES 1:23: *For if any be a hearer of the word and not a doer; he is like unto a man beholding his natural face in a glass.*

1 JOHN 3:18: *Little children, let us not love in word or talk, but in deed and in truth.*

COLOSSIANS 3:23–24: *Whatever you do, work heartily, as for the Lord and not for men, knowing that from the Lord you will receive the inheritance as your reward. You are serving the Lord Christ.*

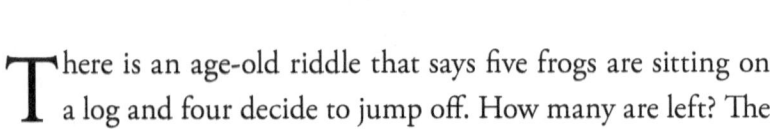

There is an age-old riddle that says five frogs are sitting on a log and four decide to jump off. How many are left? The answer is five, because nothing happens when you decide—only when an action is taken.

The philosophy for my companies is that a poor plan in motion beats a great plan on the table, every time. This should seem obvious, but I have seen many times where teams spend countless hours coming up with an elaborate plan that gets so bogged down with "to dos" that it never gets implemented. You must be able to put the rubber to the road, the boots on the ground . . . you catch my drift. If an apocalypse hit, I would rather have an old beat-up car with tires than a nice shiny car with none.

I learned a valuable lesson early in my physical therapy career. When treating patients' poststroke, it is imperative that you distinguish between movement and purposeful movement. If a patient moved their hand but they were not trying to, or they were not following directions with the movement, then that was not considered purposeful. This distinction is especially important because purposeful movement demonstrates improvement, while nonpurposeful movement demonstrates a functional plateau. This same distinction should be applied to your own actions. Are they purposeful? You cannot confuse motion with

CHAPTER II: ACTION

effectiveness. If you are like me, it is not too hard to get terribly busy doing the wrong things.

I had a physics professor who taught me a principle that I have applied throughout my entire adult life. He taught me that no matter how complex the problem, the most important thing is to start working on it. He said that you did not need to know the answer or exactly how you will get to it, but you did need to start drawing or writing the problem out. He said that as you get your brain going, you gain clarity and will start progressing toward the solution.

Ralph Waldo Emerson showed that he believed this way too when he asserted, "An ounce of action is worth a world of theory."

I remember hearing a story where a math student came to class late and there were three problems written on the board, so he copied them down for homework. He came in the next day and handed in his work. The teacher looked at his work in astonishment and told him that the three problems on the board were three problems that had never been solved, and that he had just solved them. Since the student thought these problems were only normal homework, he did not set any limitations on himself and he simply started working on them and was able to solve them.

I do not know if this story is true or not, but I do know the principle is true. Imagine how many people would never even attempt to solve those three problems because they had a mindset that the problems were unsolvable, so they did not even try. Just looking at the problem and knowing they had never been solved kept them from acting. The first step in any success plan is to simply act! John F. Kennedy was quoted as saying, "There are risks and costs to taking action, but they are far less than the long-range risks of comfortable inaction."

You do not want to fall victim to "the paralysis of analysis." Here are five things you should know about action:

1. You will never know all the answers.

2. The conditions will never be perfect.

3. There will always be people that tell you that you cannot do it.

4. Make sure the risks are within your tolerance level.

5. It is okay to crawl before you walk. Small actions are sometimes better than jumping in with both feet.

CHAPTER II: ACTION

Play 11
ACTION

1. Be sure to monitor your daily actions. Ask yourself if they are purposeful or not.

2. Write down everything you do each day for one week and approximately how long each task took. Look back and highlight any action that moved you toward one of your goals in the five focus areas. Then add up the time for any action items not highlighted, to see how much more time could have been allocated to the attainment of your goals. Be sure to note social media, TV, driving, etc. Be specific. If you are listening to an educational audio book while you are driving, then you may be able to highlight it as education! The most important thing is to be honest with yourself. You are only cheating yourself if you are not honest.

CHAPTER 12
TIME MASTERY

EPHESIANS 5:15–16: *See then that ye walk circumspectly, not as fools but as wise, redeeming the time, because the days are evil.*

PSALMS 90:12: *So teach us to number our days, that we may apply our hearts unto wisdom.*

*"This is the key to time management—
to see the value of every moment."*
—MENACHEM SCHNEERSON,
ORTHODOX RABBI AND ONE OF THE MOST INFLUENTIAL
JEWISH LEADERS OF THE 20TH CENTURY

> *"Time is the great equalizer: govern it, or it will govern you."*
> —Kevin Pyles

There is no shortage of time management books out there, most of which will have some sort of to-do list. To-do lists are a handy tool, as long as you know what not to do. To-do lists should not be the core of your strategy, because they are not motivating or energy-creating. It has been said that time is just a perception, and I think adopting this belief is the best approach to managing time. Albert Einstein summed it up pretty well by saying, "When you sit with a nice girl for two hours you think it's only a minute, but when you sit on a hot stove for a minute, you think it's two hours. That's relativity."

When you are doing something boring, doesn't it seem like it lasts forever? But if you are doing something you love, time seems to fly.

Here are my ten rules for time:

1. Govern time or it will govern you.

2. Decide, ahead of time, where you will spend your time, or you will be "time broke," in no time.

3. Do not let others spend your time.

4. Time is not money; it is much more than money.

5. There will most likely come a time in your life, where you would give anything for a little more of it.

CHAPTER 12: TIME MASTERY

6. Time, like money, needs to be invested well.

7. Your present time is of higher currency than your future time.

8. Time is a perception, so if you change your perception you change your time.

9. Quality time with those you love is the most precious form of time.

10. There are no refunds or exchanges with time, so spend it wisely.

John Wooden, the famed, winningest coach of UCLA, once said, "If you don't have time to do it right the first time, when will you ever have time to do it again?"

Let us discuss these ten rules for time in more detail.

1. Govern time or it will govern you.

When I was a kid, I remember my grandfather telling me, "If you want something done, then give it to a busy person." At that time, I did not have a clue what he meant, but boy, I do now. Busy people generally find a way to get things done, where someone with nothing to do probably is not prioritizing, and will most likely never get to it. If you are like me, there is never any shortage of stuff to do. I could not imagine trying to gain success and happiness without first understanding how to govern time.

There is a significant difference in being busy versus being effective. Being in motion does not mean you are being effective. Sure, you may be busy . . . but are you busy doing the things that must be done to achieve your dreams? I once had a manager that was a great person, but really fell behind when it came to strategic thinking and planning. When we would discuss this, he would assure me that he was busy, and there were not enough minutes in the day to get to the tasks I was asking about. I had him do an exercise which has served me well for anyone who is wanting to get a starting point for time management. I had him start a "time journal" for one week, where he recorded everything he did from the time he got to work until the time he finished his shift. I assured him that there were no "wrong things" unless they did not happen, and to simply record the truth no matter how big or small. I told him that we would review this together and develop a plan from there.

After the week had passed, we sat down together and reviewed his journal, and what we found was very eye-opening. This guy was extremely busy, but at all the wrong things. He was supposed to be a general manager, but was the best custodian and customer service rep that we had in the company. The things that he was doing were great things, but he had support staff in place to handle those tasks. He was not utilizing his staff appropriately. Rather than developing a good training program for his support staff, delegating tasks, and then monitoring

CHAPTER 12: TIME MASTERY

them, he just did everything himself, because it seemed easier than going back and fixing things.

You have probably heard the old saying, "If you want something done right, then do it yourself." That saying should be, "If you want something done right, then train someone right." By the end of the day, he had zero time and energy left to do the general manager tasks that needed to be done. I explained to him that he could not be the helmsman of the ship and be below shoveling the coal. To make it worse, this manager was on a profit-sharing plan and was working harder to make less.

2. **Decide ahead of time, where you will spend your time, or you will be "time broke" in no time.**

It is imperative that you prioritize the things that must be done in order to achieve your dreams and do them first. This will ensure you stay moving in the right direction. If you do not do this, there is a good chance that you will simply get "caught up" in the day-to-day grind and not get to the things that propel you toward your dreams. I remember a sales manager that would wait until the end of the month to scramble to try to make up missed benchmarks. He would do the right activities, but in the wrong order! We had a discussion that went like this:

"What is your most important asset?" I asked.

"Time," he said.

"Okay, then take the first twenty to thirty minutes of each day to plan your use of it and review how you used it the day before," I recommended. We called this implementing the "shot clock." When the shot clock is on, a team must be 100 percent focused on reaching the goal. When your shot clock is on, you must be 100 percent focused on reaching your goals.

He was not too keen on doing this because he thought he would be wasting another thirty minutes, but I explained the Pareto Principle, or 80/20 rule. These rules suggest that 20 percent of your time will most likely give you 80 percent of your results. With this being the case, it is imperative that you spend it right. I reference this principle knowing it may not be applicable to every situation, but being aware of its potential is still very useful.

I instructed this manager to look at which activities were driving the success of the business, and to be sure to block time for those activities first. I ended by telling him to set a block of time near the end of his day to do mundane tasks like returning nonurgent calls and emails.

Making these small changes increased this manager's numbers by 25 percent in the first month, and he went on to be one of the best managers we ever had.

3. **Do not let others spend your time.**

This is a hard lesson to learn. As the owner of a business, everyone is fighting for some of your time, whether it be employees, vendors, family, etc. Some may be warranted and some not so much. They may be trying to sell you a product, service, or idea, tell you about a problem, show you what they have been doing, or just want to spend

CHAPTER 12: TIME MASTERY

time with you. Even if this is innocent, it does not make it any less detrimental to your success.

I want you to think of this in two ways. First, if someone interrupts your day, it is like letting them reach into your wallet and take out some cash. I know you would not allow someone to just reach in your wallet and take some cash. So why would you do it with your time?

Secondly, I want you to think of each day like going on a long hike. You have a backpack filled with all the necessities to make your hike a success and ensure you reach your destination. If someone presents you with a problem with no solutions, it is like you are allowing them to remove one necessity from your backpack and replace it with a brick. It will not be long before you are bogged down with all the extra weight and will be lacking the necessities you needed to get you where you were going.

If you begin to think of problems in this way, you will greatly improve your quality of life and greatly improve the speed at which you will reach your dreams.

Here is an example of how I handle this in my own company: I am in my office during a block of time specifically used for strategic thinking for my physical therapy company. My assistant knows to "guard the fort," so to speak, to prevent interruptions. My assistant steps away from her desk inadvertently, allowing a provider relations staff member to knock on my door. I invite her in, and she tells me that I should lower the new patient benchmark for facility "x" because they are consistently missing the mark. Now, there was a time when I would mistakenly have said: "Okay, thanks, I will look into this," but experience has taught me to not accept the brick, and to keep their hand out of my wallet.

I replied by saying, "Thanks for bringing this to my attention. Here is what I need you to do:

a. Complete a twelve-month referral trend analysis for facility "x" and then compare the last three months with the same period last year.

b. Identify the top five referral sources for facility "x" and compare their referral patterns for the same periods referenced above.

c. Meet with the site manager of facility "x" and review your findings and identify the three most logical reasons for the change in volumes.

d. Discuss those findings with the Chief Operations Officer, to jointly decide if the benchmarks should be lowered or if we need a different strategy to get the numbers back up. If you decide to lower the benchmarks, then the COO needs to do an analysis of what expenses need to be cut to maintain the facility's profitability margin.

e. Email me the final documents, and I will review and either sign off or schedule a follow-up meeting for all to discuss. (I later created a "problem snapshot report" to keep this process black-and-white. I have inserted an overview of this report, along with the reason for each section, so you can create your own).

CHAPTER 12: TIME MASTERY

At first blush, it may appear that I gave her a ton of work, but I really did three things. I taught her to perform due diligence when looking at a problem and to look at data in a more comprehensive way. I taught her that when bringing me a problem, you had better include possible solutions. I allowed myself to stay focused on the things I needed to keep the company successful.

Problem Snapshot Report
Date: (Provides a start time to monitor resolution)
Problem presenter: (Provides ownership and accountability)
Problem name: (Makes it real)
Problem brief description: (Provides clarity)
Due diligence: (Ensures all necessary information has been gathered to allow for an informed decision. This can be attached to the document as it may be reports pulled from several places.)
Possible solutions: (Ensures the problem presenter has vetted the problem and put thought equity into a possible solution)
Discussed with one-up manager: ( ) Yes ( ) No
Joint assessment: (Provides opinions on problem and ramifications after discussing with one-up manager)
Proposed resolution date: (Provides a timeline to resolution)
Date sent to decision maker: (Provides timeline for final decision)
Final decision: (Provides record of the decision)

4. **Time is not money; it is much more than money.**

   This seems obvious when you stop and think about it, but I think that, in everyday life, money appears to be the most important thing in your life because you have so many reminders of it. Reminders through bills, wallets, purses, debit cards, needs, wants, etc. Could you imagine if you had receipts of everywhere you spent your time and filed each one under "goal serving" or "wasted." Wasted-time receipts would be for things like social media, TV, surfing the web, video games, and so on. What would your files look like? Would you have abundant receipts for wasted time?

   I like to think of it like this; you would give your last bit of money if it would give you more time, but you wouldn't give your last bit of time if it would give you more money. So, live your life that way.

   I did the "time receipt book" with my kids. I picked up a receipt book at the local office-supply store and had them write receipts for where they spent their time each day for one week. Then we put the receipts into two files; one for "goal serving" and the other for "wasted." This process accomplishes two things: first, they can get a visual on how their time affects their future; and second, they get a reminder that they are spending a valuable asset. This is a great exercise for adults too! (hint . . . hint . . .)

   A few facts about time as your most valuable asset:
   - You can always make more money, but you cannot make more time.
   - Once time is lost, it can never be found.

CHAPTER 12: TIME MASTERY

- You are always spending time, whether you want to or not.
- Your minutes are like workers, and they are either moving you toward your dreams or sabotaging them. Remember this acronym.

T.I.M.E.
T=Time
I=Is
M=My
E=Equalizer

Time is the one thing you have that is exactly equal to everyone else's. Everyone gets twenty-four hours per day. It is how you spend it that counts.

5. **There will most likely come a time in your life, where you would give anything for a little more of it.**

If you only had a few days to live, and were offered a million dollars that only you could spend, or a thousand more healthy days, what would you choose?

I look at it like this: time equals opportunity. Isn't that what it is? You can change your whole life in a mere second. The second you decide, things change. Time is an opportunity to grow, to learn, to love, to forgive, and to accomplish.

"Time will eventually demand the respect it always deserved."
—KEVIN PYLES

6. **Time, like money, needs to be invested well.**

We touched on this a bit in numbers three and four. There is no shortage of people wanting to help you invest your money, but where are the people wanting to help you invest your time? I encountered this problem early in my business career. I allowed my sales staff at my health club to start doing personal training occasionally. It was not long before sales started to decline, and the overall membership numbers at the club declined. Here is the mistake I made, using hypothetical numbers:

Let us say the salesman made $10 an hour as a base pay and was on a tiered-commission system that looked like this:

Base Pay: $10 per hour, and should sell 1 to 9 memberships per month.
Commission
Level 1: Sales of 10 to 19 memberships per month.
   Commission is 15 percent of total monthly fees.
Level 2: Sales of 20 to 29 memberships per month.
   Commission is 20 percent of total monthly fees.
Level 3: Sales of 30 or more memberships per month.
   Commission is 50 percent of total monthly fees.

If you reach Level 3 for 3 months in a row, your base pay will go up 50 cents, permanently.

Personal Training: The facility charged $40 and gave the trainer 40 percent or $16 per session, with no base pay during that hour. We made the mistake of letting

CHAPTER 12: TIME MASTERY

sales staff train members, if desired. The staff thought, "Why make $10 per hour when I can make $16 per hour?" Once I noticed that sales were dropping because staff was not on the sales floor due to training, I tried to explain that, with the training, they were putting a ceiling on their earning potential. If they did personal training for 40 hours a week, which would have been very unlikely, but if they could, they would make a maximum of $640. This number would always be reduced because of cancels and no-shows. There is no base pay during this time, because it was scheduled as personal training time.

With the sales if they worked 40 hours, their base pay would be $400. If they had forty sales averaging $60, their commission would have been 50 percent of $2,400 or $1,200. This gives them a total weekly salary of $400+$1,200, which is $1,600. If they made Level 3 every month, then their base would go up $2.00 per hour annually ($.50 x 4). If they worked hard on the front end, in five years they would have a $20 per hour base salary and still get commission.

The system was designed to be front-end loaded, meaning I wanted to hire winners that knew how to work hard first to have security down the road. It was difficult for the staff to see past the current hour they were in. If I had let this continue, they would have trained us right out of business. The problem was that this plan was designed for "go getters" not "go takers." Needless to say, we made some changes. The moral of the story is that you cannot just look at the short-term, but must look at the big picture.

I think four of the best ways to invest your time are learning, relationships/meeting new people, giving back, and loving.

7. **Your present time is of higher currency than your future time.**

    I have met many businessmen who fell into this trap. They worked themselves to death by always chasing the future, only to one day realize they never caught it. They forgot to enjoy the ride. You must have a balance and know what you are shooting for. I might have fallen victim to this had I not read several books in which I was advised of this trap. I think planning for the future like you will live forever, while living like there is no tomorrow, is a great way to live.

    As I started my career as a physical therapist, I worked in a hospital. There I talked with many people that were extremely sick or dying. Most of them said things like; "Son, if I had known I was going to end up like this, I would have done 'x' when I was younger." They would say, "Do not wait to do things you want to do; do them now while you can!" Basically, the message was, do not put off doing things with those you love until "someday," because when "someday" gets here, you may not be able.

8. **Time is just a perception; so if you change your perception you can change your time.**

CHAPTER 12: TIME MASTERY

Remember Einstein's quote. "When you sit with a nice girl for two hours you think it's only a minute, but when you sit on a hot stove for a minute, you think it's two hours. That's relativity." Please note there are several variations of this quote, but it does not matter. The principle is all you are after here. If time is a perception and you control your perception, then you can control your time. As we discussed in our chapter on focus, if you focus on the wrong things and keep yourself in a state of stress and anxiety, then you will never seem to have enough time. This can inadvertently happen with a poorly designed to-do list. If you just have a list of things to do, without strategically relating them back to your goals and dreams, then you can be busy, stressed, and never seem to have enough time, all while not progressing toward your dreams.

I believe the best way to feel like you have enough time is to ensure all daily tasks be causally related to your goals. By doing this, you will always be moving toward your dreams and creating the future God intended for you. This way, it is not a catastrophe if you do not cross off every task, because the ones you did cross off will be moving you toward your dreams.

There will always be tasks that seem like "time takers" that may be a missed opportunity. For example, if one of my goals in relationships is to make my kids feel loved and supported, then taking them to soccer practice could be repurposed to serve these goals. Instead of thinking that I must take thirty minutes to fight traffic to get across town, I can think of a productive way to use this time with them. I could creatively discuss a habit of winners in an age-appropriate way. I could tell them about a mistake I made when I was young, and how I am smarter now. We could discuss some of the positive character traits they have and how proud they make their mom and me. I like to finish these types of discussions by asking them why they think I am telling them about it.

You could also use this time to ask your kids about their day, or to see if they have anything they would like to discuss. Kids are much smarter than most people give them credit for, especially with emotional intelligence. Your children will realize that you are talking to them because you love and want the best for them. They know if you are too busy for them and on your phone while they are just riding in the back. This is why kids often look to video games for stimulation. Now, you took 30 minutes to work on making your kids feel loved and supported, instead of spending 30 minutes on something irrelevant. If you adopt this mindset and be sure that on each day most of your tasks are linked back to your goals, you will stay more relaxed and feel in better control of your time.

9. **Quality time with those you love is the most precious form of time.**

How do you know this? Just give it the "death-bed" test. I know we do not like to think about that, but sometimes we need to. If you had one day left to live, who would you spend it with? I can assure you that there is no business

CHAPTER 12: TIME MASTERY

deal that is more precious than your spouse or children. I can also assure you that there is no amount of money that you can leave to loved ones that would be more valuable to them than quality time with you while you are here. Have you ever noticed that people who have had a near-death experience always seem to get the most out of life and often have the best attitudes? They try to find happiness in every moment, no matter what. This is because they are grateful, and they realize the true value of that thing we call time.

Always keep in mind that it is not the quantity of time but the quality of time that counts. Ten minutes holding your spouse's hand and looking into their eyes is worth more than an hour of you sitting in a chair watching TV while they are on the sofa. I always say, "Relationships fed on scraps, die first." I teach my executives this philosophy as well. So many businesspersons treat their clients and colleagues great, only to go home so tired and exhausted that their family gets the worst of them. How many lives have been ruined by this?

Many years ago, I adopted a practice that I think everyone should be using. I alluded to this technique in an early chapter. I define the result I would like to have in every interaction I have with another person. For example, if I call someone on my leadership team, I may set a goal to not only discuss the week's agenda, but also to make sure I make them feel appreciated and good about themselves by the time the call ends. If I talk with my wife in the morning before I leave for work, I may have a goal to not only tell her goodbye, but also to make her feel beautiful and loved before I head out the door. This may seem to be a daunting task at first, but trust me you will be doing this consistently in no time at all.

This practice is not just for people you know, either. I do this with the call to the cable company, the clerk at the corner store, etc. I may define the result to be that I would like to spread some cheer and make the person laugh before ending the conversation. Making someone else's day a little better gives me momentum in my own day. I should also note here that since time with those we love is the most precious time we have, it is very important to know what love means to each of those people.

No one describes this better than Dr. Gary Chapman in his book, *The Five Love Languages*, where he contends the five ways to express heartfelt commitment are: gifts, quality time, words of affirmation, acts of service, and physical touch. I read this book when I first got married, not because my marriage needed help, but because I had never been married, and I wanted to make sure that I stayed that way. I knew divorce rates were high and rising. I figured I was not immune, so I did what I always do: have a faith in God and then do my part. The neat thing about Dr. Chapman's theory is that you can apply it to all relationships, and not just a spouse.

It works great with children too. Just ask your child what you do that makes them know you love them. That answer will be the language you need to speak to your child to make him or her feel loved. There is more to it,

CHAPTER 12: TIME MASTERY

so you should read the book and apply the knowledge to your life. This book will help ensure that you protect the most important relationships while working toward your dreams.

10. **There are no refunds or exchanges with time, so spend it right the first time.**

I cannot think of one elderly person that I have ever talked to that said life sure seems to have gone by slow. I would wager that anyone reading this book has heard older folks say, "Boy, time sure does fly." or "The older we get, the faster it seems to have gone." That is because time really is just a perception. The time you are in right now will one day be time that flew by, so use it wisely and enjoy every minute!

While doing any nonessential task, you should look for two or three things that you can do at the same time. A nonessential task is a task that does not require your 100 percent undivided attention. I call this "double-time." It is important to note that this is not multitasking. Multitasking does not work. Research has shown that multitasking is just task switching, and there are increased risks of mistakes and time wasted with refocusing. Here are some examples of how I apply double-time to my life:

a. Listening to audio books while driving in the car (education + getting where I need to go)

b. Stretching, while performing breathing exercises, while listening to audio books (flexibility/circulation + health/relaxation + education)

c. Performing calisthenics/weightlifting with my wife and kids (exercise + family time)
d. Horse riding with my wife (exercise + time in nature + time with spouse)
e. Listening to a sermon while mowing (spirituality + chore completion)
f. Stretching on my rest breaks when lifting weights (flexibility + strength)

You can see how small changes create more time for you and can keep you on track toward goal attainment. When I hear people complain about having to drive an hour or getting stuck in traffic for 30 minutes, I feel bad for them. This never bothers me because I always have audiobooks available. If I am in the car for a while, whether planned or not, it provides me more opportunity to learn. I am always looking for opportunities for double-time.

I debated whether to include this next section, but I am going to throw it in. This may seem crazy, but I have noticed over the years of hiring hundreds of people that the ones who walk with a slow gait with their shoulders tipped backward or slouched with a backward lean never seem to be good time managers and usually end up in the bottom 10 percent of productivity or effectiveness. I know, I used to think I was crazy too, but it happened over and over again. It happened to the point that I could no longer deny it. The employees who walked upright, forward-leaning with a faster gait always came out on the high end of productivity. Now, there are always exceptions

CHAPTER 12: TIME MASTERY

and, of course, this may not apply if there is a disability or functional limitation involved but start looking in your own company/life and see if you don't find this pattern to be true. You may need to check your own walk!

Now that you understand all the different aspects of time, let us look at how I like to govern it. I developed a time management system that I call, "All-Star Time Management." I purposefully kept this system simple and concise. This system uses the analogy of a basketball game to provide a visual reference. The game is your focus area. Each focus area consists of a ball (your tasks), shot clock (daily planning time), boundary lines (reminders to stay in the game), goal (what you are trying to obtain), all-star players (the best people to help you reach the goal), and a 3-point line (the priority items that will give you the most return).

In this game, we play with several balls instead of just one. This is because you have more than one task per day. The first thing to happen when a team gets the ball is that the shot clock comes on. When the shot clock is on, the players are focused and begin running plays to allow them to get to the goal in a given amount of time. As soon as you begin your workday you turn your shot clock on by taking no more than 20 to 30 minutes to plan your day in blocks of time. You should think of each block of time like a separate quarter in the game. Be sure to plan your day while your "goals" are watching. What I mean is, be sure the blocks of time consist of the things that will move you toward your goals. Each day, you move toward the goal in each quarter of the game (focus areas). You need to run your best plays first. Your best plays are always the ones that give you the most points (best return). We call these our 3-point plays. In this game, we never miss the basket; we just keep working until we get the ball to the goal. Each ball (task) gets a letter an A-B-C type of system which correlates it to the primary focus area. If the letter is written in **bold**, then it is a 3-point play and is a priority item. If it is a normal font, it is still valuable, but should typically not come before the 3-point plays have been run. I draw a circle around the letter for anything that has a rigid time which cannot be moved. Examples of rigid time would be my morning vision quest/ritual or a critical meeting with someone. Remember to utilize the if/then philosophy for things that must happen. The boundary lines are just a mental image to remind you to stay in the game. I write things outside the boundary lines at the end of each day, like unexpected things that pop up. A flat tire, for example. I have included a fictitious example of a day at the end of this chapter. This will take you some time in the beginning, but do not give up on it. You will get faster as you get accustomed to it, and will eventually only spend about 20 minutes on it.

Please note, it is not imperative that you use the same system as I do. There are many good systems out there, but you must do the research. You must understand and enjoy using whatever system you choose. Consistency is the key here.

CHAPTER 12: TIME MASTERY

Play 12

TIME MASTERY

1. Implement the All-Star Time Management System, particularly the Daily Shot Clock to start your day with organization and intent. Remember, you do not have to mark off all your "to dos," just be sure that the blocks of time are moving you toward your goals. You can carry over any items that you did not get to, to the next day, without feeling guilty or anxious, because overall, you have moved toward your goals and dreams.

2. Develop your decision-making tree in an if/then fashion. Be sure to explain and train your key subordinates on its use. If you do not have anyone under you, then just use the system as it may apply to you.

3. List three to five things you currently do on a regular basis that are not serving your goals. Commit to stop doing those things for 30 days and reallocate that time to things that serve your goals. Once you have seen the progress you can make, you will not go back to the old time-wasters!

THE DIVINE PLAYBOOK

(EXAMPLE: ALL STAR TIME MANAGEMENT)

Here is a sample:
Focus areas: Spirituality/Family/Financial
Date: January 1, 20xx
Spirituality:

A) **Primary Goal:** To feel a 10/10 connection with God by April 1, 20xx while living in awe.

Action Goals:

1. Spend seven minutes per day in devotions, starting at 5:50 a.m. consisting of repentance, Bible reading, and a prayer to implement and manifest the scripture.

2. Listen to gospel music daily during an organic lunch. (double-time—spirituality and health)

3. Volunteer at Children's Home Society every Wednesday at 7:00 p.m.

B) **Primary Goal:** To have a 10/10 connection with my wife and children by April 1, 20xx while living in awe.

Action Goals:

1. Exercise with my wife and children Monday, Wednesday, and Friday morning at 7:30 a.m. for one hour, while

making sure they know I love them. (double-time—health and relationships)

2. Sit with my wife daily and pray for her out loud for three to five minutes at 9:00 p.m.

3. Do at least one individual activity per week for a minimum of one hour with each of my children.

4. Go on at least one date every four weeks with my wife, in which it is only her and me.

C) Primary Goal: Have a minimum of $50,000 in an emergency savings account by June 1, 20xx while living in awe.

1. Cancel all luxury expenses such as cable, extra cell phones, unnecessary gas/travel, eating out, and others by January 10, 20xx and put that recurring money into savings.

2. Increase sales by 20 percent by June 1, 20xx by making twenty phone calls per day to prospective buyers while maintaining a closing ratio of 65 percent and put the additional revenue generated into savings.

3. Set a weekly staff meeting with managers every Friday at 3:00 p.m. to review the weekly KPIs for each store, to ensure we achieve established benchmarks each month.

THE DIVINE PLAYBOOK

Now, let's look at an example of a day:

ALL-STAR TIME MANAGEMENT DATE: XX/XX/XXXX

5:30 a.m.: Shot Clock (A,B,C)

5:50 a.m.: Scripture (A)

(6:00 a.m.:) Daily Vision Quest (C)

7:00 a.m.: Workout with wife and kids (B)

8:00 a.m.: Product—research and development (C)

9:00 a.m.: Research and make 20 phone calls for business (C)

10:00 a.m.: Call to cancel "luxury expense accounts" (C)

11:00 a.m.: Hike with daughter in woods (B)

12:15 p.m.: Organic lunch/water with Randy Travis gospel album (A)

1:00 p.m.: Read personal development/business literature (C)

Moved to next day because electric dog fence broke and had to fix it

2:00 p.m.: Review business benchmarks and travel to facility (Listen to motivational sermon while traveling) (A) (C) [with travel—double-time]

CHAPTER 12: TIME MASTERY

3:00 p.m.: Meet with managers (make sure each one feels valued) (C)

4:00 p.m.: Travel (continue sermon and have healthy snack / water (A) [with travel—double-time]

4:30 p.m.: Return important calls and emails (C)

5:30 p.m.: Sit in nature /Relax/Meditate (A) (B)

7:00 p.m.: Volunteer at Children's Home Society with my kids (A) (B) [double-time]

8:00 p.m.: Family supper at table (Make each child feel heard and important. Creatively discuss one mistake I made and how I handled it or one success I had as a young adult.) (B)

9:00 p.m.: Pray with wife (A) (B)

9:15 p.m.: Tuck kids in bed and pray with them (A) (B)

10:00 p.m.: Write in gratitude journal/perform incantations and relax for bed (A)(B)(C)

CHAPTER 13
HABITS

1 CORINTHIANS 6:12: *"All things are lawful unto me, but all things are not expedient: all things are lawful for me, but I will not be brought under the power of any."*

ROMANS 12:2: *Do not conform to the patterns of this world, but be transformed by the renewing of your mind, that ye may prove what is that good, and acceptable, and perfect, will of God.*

1 CORINTHIANS 10:13: *No temptation has overtaken you except what is common to mankind. And God is faithful; he will not let you be tempted beyond what you can bear. But when you are tempted, he will also provide a way out so that you can endure it.*

> "You make your habits one day at a time,
> then they make you for a lifetime."
> —Kevin Pyles

> "We become what we repeatedly do."
> —Sean Covey

> "Your net worth to the world is usually determined by what remains after your bad habits are subtracted from your good ones."
> —Benjamin Franklin

As each of these biblical secrets were revealed to me, I found myself wanting to proclaim each to be one of the most important things on the path to success. The reason for this is because they are all so intertwined. It takes the synergism of all these principles, working in divine harmony, to accomplish a goal. One, or even a few, of these principles will fall short if left without the synergies of the entire program.

Think of habits like a coin. A coin has two sides. Just like the coin there are two sides to habits. There are good habits, and on the other side bad habits. Your subconscious mind does not score the habit or put it in one of those categories; it simply runs the program installed. There is a common problem that I have found with most folks aligning their habits with their goals. Their goals are set with their conscious mind, and they do good for a few weeks or maybe months, but then they seem to fall off and back into old unsuccessful patterns.

Why is this? I believe that we set goals with our conscious mind, but must attain them with our subconscious mind,

CHAPTER 13: HABITS

because that is where our habits dwell. The first example that comes to mind is New Year's resolutions. They typically start off great, but then over 90 percent of the time falter within a few months. Owning a health club for over twenty years gave me plenty of exposure to this phenomenon. The problem is that you get excited and set a goal, and as long as you hold it in your consciousness, you do well. But then, as your willpower tires, your subconscious mind takes over and runs the programs of your old daily habits. This frustrating cycle leads you right back to the place that you so desperately wanted out of. This is because you have not done the work to program the new goal—serving habits into your subconscious mind.

You may have heard that it takes twenty-one days to twenty-six days or maybe some other magic number to change a habit, but I am not convinced that you can put a number on it. I believe there are many variables to habits, and it would be difficult to put an exact time required to change them. Variables like is it physical, chemical, or both? How long has your habit been embedded? How strong is your current willpower? How committed are you to changing the habit? What is your current environment? Do you have a good strategy in place to replace the bad habit with a good habit? All these variables can greatly affect the process of change.

It is vitally important to develop habits and rituals that are in direct alignment with your goals and dreams. In order to change a habit, you must first define what a habit is, and then must be consciously aware of a given habit. In a nutshell, a habit is nothing more than a subconscious program running in the background of your mind. You can think of it like a program you install on your computer. Once installed, the program is always there to help you accomplish or in some cases not accomplish a task. You need not know exactly how the program works, because once installed, you can simply plug in data and let the program do its job.

Likewise, if you have a bad program, like a virus, it will also run in the background, wreaking havoc on your computer system. You should think of your bad programming like a computer virus. You have bad programming that is quietly running in the background, manifesting nonserving habits, eventually derailing you from your goals. The science is clear here. I always say to my students: "Conquer your habits or they will conquer you." I have heard it said that habits take the short-term work of your conscious mind and turn it into the long-term work of your subconscious mind, and I have to agree.

I believe that many bad habits are formed as a short-term fix to a negative emotional state. For example, you get bored or you are stressed, so you have some junk food and a soda to give you something to do in an attempt to make yourself feel better temporarily. This may seem to work at first, but eventually it can have significant health consequences. Another example would be simple things like hitting the snooze button on your alarm clock. It starts off innocently, with you trying to catch a few more "Zs," but eventually can lead to you dreading mornings and feeling sluggish upon awakening. The sleep during the last few snooze button hits is generally not restful sleep anyway.

"*Those that don't start early have to trot all day.*"—Ben Franklin

I believe it is imperative to have a good "start of the day" habit. I started a morning ritual that I call my morning "vision

CHAPTER 13: HABITS

quest." I derived this term from Native American Indians who used vision quests to find themselves and their life's direction. I liked this term because I feel like the way we start each day has a profound effect on our life's direction and who we are, or are to become. It is imperative that once you implement a morning ritual, you stick to it no matter what. You must hop out of bed and get straight to the first task in your ritual, so you do not start convincing yourself of why staying in bed would be better. Just wake up and get going! Some like to do the countdown principle, where they say, "five, four, three, two, one, and jump out of bed.

Here is an example of my morning Vision Quest: (all times are approximate and may vary according to need)

1. Awaken: I hit the floor and take an ice-cold rinse in the shower. (three to five minutes)

2. Scripture: I spend time with God, which consists of praying for wisdom, and studying a scripture. (five to seven minutes)

3. Breathing: I get outside, face east toward the sunrise, and take ten deep breaths while extending my arms overhead, and then five regular breaths, and say, "Man, it feels good to be alive" three times. (three minutes)

4. Motion with Emotion: I jog with a strong and confident posture, while breathing in on a four-to-five count and breathing out on a long, slow breath (usually an eight count). (five minutes)

5. Gratitude: I give a passionate prayer of thanks for the things I am thankful for. All the blessings in my life and give thanks that I am achieving my goals. This removes all fear for the day. (ten minutes)

6. Mind-movie: Play your mind-movie while talking through it. In this program, you will have created a "mind-movie" that is only about three to five minutes in length. Play this movie over and over feeling the joy and accomplishment that this movie represents. (five to ten minutes)

7. Incantations and recorded affirmations. While continuing jogging, I chant loudly the incantations that I created, or I listen to the recorded affirmations from my loved ones. I usually have three to five incantations that I really like, and often change them up. I chant these in a rhythmic manner, so they will be "catchy" and easily adopted by my subconscious mind. One of my favorites is, "I can do an-y-thing . . . my dreams will come true!" (ten minutes to one hour)

Do not get bogged down with the times; just do what you can. If you only have ten minutes one day, then shorten everything to complete it all in that amount of time. I do, however, try to complete each section, if only for a minute.

Now let us discuss the "other side of the coin," the bad habit side. It is important to identify any nonserving habits you may have and replace them with goal-serving habits. There are basically seven keys to change a habit:

CHAPTER 13: HABITS

1. Identify the habit.

2. Pray for the change and accept it as accomplished.

3. Keep it in your conscious mind.

4. Change the underlying supporting belief.

5. Identify what new habit the old habit will be replaced with.

6. Tell your Divine Mind what your new habit will be and thank it for already manifesting the new habit.

7. Practice the new habit; be consistent and be patient.

Play 13
HABITS

1. Identify one to three nonserving habits and plan to deal with them one at a time.

2. Start with the habit that you feel is most greatly hindering your success.

3. Follow the seven keys to change a habit.

4. If you feel comfortable doing so, tell someone you trust about the habit you are changing, and ask them to hold you accountable.

5. Reference the belief chapter here, as they are intimately intertwined.

CHAPTER 14
COMMUNICATION

MATTHEW 12:37: *For by thy words thou shalt be justified, and by thy words thou shalt be condemned.*

JAMES 1:19: *My dear brothers and sisters, take note of this: Everyone should be quick to listen, slow to speak and slow to become angry.*

EPHESIANS 4:29: *Do not let any unwholesome talk come out of your mouths, but only what is helpful for building others up according to their needs, that it may benefit those who listen.*

PROVERBS 15:1–2: *A gentle answer turns away wrath, but a harsh word stirs up anger. The tongue of the wise adorns knowledge, but the mouth of the fool gushes folly.*

PSALMS 141:3: *Set a guard over my mouth, Lord; keep watch over the door of my lips.*

COLOSSIANS 4:6: *Let your conversation be always full of grace, seasoned with salt, so that you may know how to answer everyone.*

2 TIMOTHY 2:16: *Avoid godless chatter, because those who will indulge in it will become more and more ungodly.*

PROVERBS 18:13: *To answer before listening—that is folly and shame.*

PROVERBS 18:21: *The tongue has the power of life and death, and those who love it will eat its fruit.*

PROVERBS 12:18–19: *The words of the reckless pierce like swords, but the tongue of the wise brings healing. Truthful lips endure forever, but a lying tongue lasts only a moment.*

PROVERBS 12:18: *The words of the reckless pierce like swords, but the tongue of the wise brings healing.*

"You can change your world by changing your words."
—JOEL OSTEEN

CHAPTER 14: COMMUNICATION

I believe communication is the master of all relationships, including the one you have with yourself. I included many scriptures here, to demonstrate just how important communication is. Jim Rohn, the late American entrepreneur, author, and motivational speaker, asserted, "Effective communication is 20 percent what you know and 80 percent how you feel about what you know." Research carried out by the Carnegie Institute of Technology shows that 85 percent of your financial success is due to skills in "human engineering," which include your ability to communicate, negotiate, and lead.

I think that number may even be higher if we included the communication we have with ourselves. Most of us think of communication as merely the words we say, but I believe, along with many others, that is only a minimal part. One of the most cited studies on the importance of verbal and nonverbal communication is one by Professor Albert Mehrabian of the University of California. In the 1970s, his studies suggested that we overwhelmingly deduce our feelings, attitudes, and beliefs about what someone says not by the actual words spoken, but by the speaker's body language and tone of voice. In fact, Prof. Mehrabian quantified this tendency: words, tone of voice, and body language respectively account for 7 percent, 38 percent, and 55 percent of personal communication.

This is one reason that I am incredibly careful with electronic communication. It is quite easy for someone to misinterpret the true meaning of a message because of the absence of tone and body language which accounts for 93 percent of the message. Mark Twain summed it up perfectly when he said, "Words are only a painted fire; a look is the fire itself." Twain is saying that while words will tell a small part of the story, the facial expressions and body language will reveal the whole story. I always tell my children two things when it comes to crucial conversations:

1. Always have them face to face.

2. Listen with your eyes first and ears second.

Here is an example. Read the following statement:

You will never amount to anything.

How does that make you feel? Probably not too good, because you cannot see my face but if you could see that I was making a funny face and smiling, then you would know that I am joking. I made a game of this with my kids to teach them about body language and tone. I would make a facial expression or adopt a certain body position, and then ask them to guess the feeling I was trying to convey. Next, I would have them close their eyes, and I would say the same sentence twice, with two different tones, and they would have to pick the one that matched whatever emotion I had given them. We would also repeat all of this with them doing the actions and me guessing.

This is a great way to teach kids (adults, too, for that matter) the importance of how they use tone and body language. They make a connection through the game and become aware of how they sound when they talk with others. You can do this with writing too. WOULD YOU PLEASE READ THIS! Doesn't that make it seem more assertive? I had a manager who was from

CHAPTER 14: COMMUNICATION

another country, and every time she would email me she would put an exclamation point at the end. Finally, one day, I asked her if she was always angry or excited when she would message me. She said she was not, and that she had never really thought about it but could see how it would appear that way.

Communication falls under the topic of EQ (emotional intelligence), which I believe is more important in determining success than IQ (intellectual intelligence). Being smart does not necessarily make you an effective communicator. Many people that own a business may have people smarter than them as employees. The difference is that they know how to communicate with a broad range of people. To be a good leader, you must be a good communicator.

Another reason that makes communication so important is the fact that you can't reach success by yourself, and the only way to elicit the help from others that you will need is to be able to communicate effectively with them. When I say, "communicate effectively," I mean communicate in varying styles. You must be able to read the communication style of the person you are speaking with, in order to communicate with them in a way that will connect and make sense to them. You also must be able to read their body language, facial expressions, and tone to ensure they understood what you were trying to say and, in the way that you meant for it to come across.

A good strategy to implement to ensure that someone hears what you meant for them to hear is to simply ask them. For example, after you make a statement tell the person that you want to make sure you are expressing yourself correctly, so you would like for them to tell you what they heard you say. You can see if their body language, tone, and words match what you meant for them to hear. You will be surprised how many times what someone heard is not quite how you meant for it to come across. By using this strategy, you have a chance to restate yourself and increase the chance of a successful outcome.

This can also work in reverse. If someone says something to you that does not match the situation, then ask them the following: "So, let me make sure I'm understanding you correctly. What I'm hearing you say is . . ." I use this with my employees all the time. If an employee comes to my office to talk with me, and their body language does not match their words, I'll say, "I feel like your body language is not matching what you're saying; is there more you want to say?" There usually is! Other clarifying statements are:

"Does this make sense?"

"What are your thoughts about what I just said?"

"I want to be sure I am expressing myself correctly. What did you hear me say?"

You can improve your communication skills much faster by using clarifying statements like the ones above.

Another communication skill to master is one I call "loaded versus unloaded" communication. Loaded communication uses a word choice that could easily be misinterpreted. Just like a loaded gun can hurt you, loaded communication can hurt you. Unloaded communication is much more intent-focused, as to not give much variation in interpretation. Remember, all communication includes the three components of words, tone, and body language, as we described earlier, but we are just going to focus on word choice for this illustration. Here is an example:

You are speaking to someone, and after you state your point, you then say, "Do you understand me?" Or, "I want to be sure

CHAPTER 14: COMMUNICATION

I said this correctly; can you tell me what you heard?" Which one is loaded and just waiting to explode? I hope you picked number one.

Both number one and two could clarify what the person heard you say, but number one has a much greater chance of offending or putting someone on the defensive, with them thinking you are questioning their competence. Start paying attention to the words you choose and classifying them as loaded or unloaded.

There is no doubt the most important conversations you will ever have are the ones you have with yourself. Research shows that you can break bad habits and create happiness through learning to have better conversations with yourself. Did you know that you talk to yourself every waking hour, at a rate of approximately 600–3,000 words per minute? There are two potential problems with this.

First, most people are not even aware of this at all and if you are not aware, then you cannot make your self-communication purposeful. Second, most people tend to self-talk about negative things more than positive. This repetitive, negative self-talk becomes a negative, nonserving habit which, in turn, attracts more negative thoughts and emotions. These constant, everyday talks with yourself slowly but surely program your subconscious mind, and then it continually scans your environment for things that fit. Remember, whatever you focus on will expand.

Said differently, you will always find what you are looking for. Your subconscious mind will not distinguish between right and wrong, good or bad; it will simply follow the programs created by you. This is especially important to know, because this means that you should be having strategic conversations with yourself and choosing your words wisely. Conversations that will move you toward your goals and dreams, and not away from them.

Most ideas can be positive-focused or negative-focused. Here is an example I use with my kids. Instead of them praying, "Please God, do not let me have bad dreams," I have them say, "Please God, let me have good dreams." Now this may seem like overkill, but you start developing your word choice habits at a very young age, and in my opinion the sooner you learn to always verbalize or think of the positive side of every situation, the better off you will be. Instead of saying, "I hope I do not get sick," say, "I will stay healthy." In the first example, the subconscious mind may only hear the words "bad dreams" and, later, it may begin to recall "bad dreams." In the latter example, the subconscious mind may only hear "sick" and eventually start to bring forth emotions, symptoms, or conditions that yield sickness.

In my therapy business, it is standard in the industry to measure and benchmark missed patient appointments by cancellations and no-shows. I like to measure the other side of the equation by measuring arrival rates. Both give you the same information: 90 percent of your patients arrived today, or 10 percent did not show up today. I always prefer to focus on the positive.

The first step in creating constructive conversations with yourself is simply to be aware that you are having them. Once you are paying attention to these conversations you should begin to look at patterns of negativity and implement a strategy that I call flipping. We have already discussed this concept in a previous chapter. In this case, flipping is switching a negatively constructed statement to a positively constructed one. An example of flipping

CHAPTER 14: COMMUNICATION

would be stating, "I want to be on time," instead of stating, "I don't want to be late." There is generally always a way to flip a statement, and before long, you will be talking to yourself and others in a more positive fashion.

Did you know that the conscious mind only controls about 2 to 4 percent of what we do? That leaves a lot to the autopilot. Your brain is made up of one trillion cells with about one trillion connections between them. This means your brain could be handling ten quadrillion instructions per second! The communication you have with yourself goes a long way in the type of programs and instructions that you will use. It is not just about the words you choose either. The amount of emotion you put behind those words can have a lasting impact. The more emotion you put into a statement, the stickier it gets. In other words, it will be easier to recall and be more available when needed.

Most experts refer to this as neural anchors. Here is an example of a neural anchor: What were you doing about 8:30 a.m. and 9:00 a.m. on September 11, 2001? Most people can tell you exactly where they were and probably what they were wearing when the tragedy of the World Trade Center attacks took place. This was very emotional, and it made the thoughts and conversations you had at that time very sticky. Now, if I asked what you were doing two-and-a-half months ago on Saturday at 2:30 p.m. most people would struggle with that one, because it is very likely that there is no emotional or neural anchor associated with that time.

You can use neural anchors to your advantage by building them into your success strategy. Whenever you have a big win or a breakthrough, you will more than likely have a surge of positive emotions. When this happens, you should create a trigger to associate with this neural anchor. A trigger would be an action or verbal command which would trigger the same state of emotion as the win. An example of this would be whenever I first find out that I have closed a big deal, I will immediately clap my hands together in front of my chest and then point my arm and index finger to the sky while yelling out a profound "Vigeo." Vigeo is a Latin word that means to flourish, thrive, be effective, be strong, and be vigorous. This word has become my personal motto. I have done this so many times that now I can do this and create the emotion whenever I need it. I also do this prior to attending an important meeting. This ensures I go into the meeting projecting the energy and positive vibes associated with being a winner.

I like to call this starting your engine. Your success engine! It is important that your level of energy matches the situation. As Ecclesiastes 3:4 says, there is a time to weep, and a time to laugh; a time to mourn, and a time to dance. I take this to mean not only will there be different seasons in our life, but there is a time and place for different emotions and levels of emotion. You would not use the same RPMs to take your grandmother to church as you would for a drag race. Similarly, a meeting with the board about a sensitive issue would not warrant the same energy as a stage presentation to a group that purchased tickets. Make sense?

"Communication is the key that opens the door of opportunity."
—Kevin Pyles

CHAPTER 14: COMMUNICATION

Play 14
COMMUNICATION

1. For the next six weeks, focus on your communication. Weeks one and two, focus on physiology (body language). For weeks three and four, focus on your tone. For weeks five and six, focus on word choice considering loaded versus unloaded communication. After these six weeks you will be a more effective communicator. Just keep practicing, because you will continue to improve.

2. Be sure to include incantations, as mentioned earlier, in your morning ritual/Vision Quest.

3. For the next four weeks master the art of flipping. Monitor your self-talk/thoughts throughout the day. Every time you start to say a negative phrase, flip it to a positive one. Remember, you can use a visual picture here to make this process more effective. I like to picture the cartoon judoka running in, getting his grips on the cartoon negative phrase and flipping it to reveal the positive phrase. You can use this or come up with your own, as long as it works for you!

4. Create a speaker notebook: Over the next three months, watch at least one powerful speaker presentation per

month. You can do this online or in person. (At least one "in person" is recommended). Create a notebook and take notes on the speaker's body language, tone, verbal cadence, emotional connection/conviction, passion, syntax, and their word choice. Be aware of the crowd and what connects with them and yields a positive response. Practice, in front of a mirror, the things you found effective.

    a. Bonus: If you feel comfortable, try being part of as many speaking engagements as possible. Test yourself. Use transference here. If you can have a conversation with a friend, you can have a conversation with a large group. Just see them as a group of friends. You will get better each time, and when you need to rise to the occasion for a crucial conversation or presentation, you will!

5. Block off time on your schedule to study, practice, and research communication. You should allot a minimum of three to five hours per week until you feel extremely comfortable.

6. Mirror Technique. You can use the mirror technique as we did before on the confidence play. Practice speaking in front of a mirror; pay close attention to your body language and tone. You can also record yourself on video, play it back, and critique yourself.

CHAPTER 15
HEALTH

1 Corinthians 6:19–20: *Do you not know that your bodies are temples of the Holy Spirit, who is in you, whom you have received from God? You are not your own; you were bought at a price. Therefore, honor God with your bodies.*

1 Timothy 4:8: *For physical training is of some value, but godliness has value for all things, holding promise for both present life and the life to come.*

1 Corinthians 10:31: *So whether you eat or drink or whatever you do, do it all for the glory of God.*

> *"Unless a man dies a quick, accidental death, there will come a time in his life where he would give anything for his health back."*
> —KEVIN PYLES

Health rivals time as your most precious asset, and they are intertwined. Health may be one of the most often overlooked components of many success strategies. What good is more time or success if you are not well? Have you heard the saying: "You don't want to be the richest man in the graveyard?" Well, you do not. You can literally work yourself to death, or into a condition equal to it. One of the most important things you will ever do is to create coping strategies to offset the stress that assuredly comes with chasing your dreams. I believe the healthier and more energetic you are, the faster you can reach and enjoy your dreams. The key word being "enjoy."

I am not implying that unhealthy people cannot make money, because they do it all the time, but in most of those cases they are not fulfilled when they reach their dreams, which is the whole point. Isn't it? These people would not meet our definition of success. You cannot buy health. As you may have seen with the late, successful businessman Steve Jobs, sometimes money cannot solve your problem. This is a perfect example of why you must enjoy the process of achieving your dreams, and not try to wait until you get there.

Randy Pausch was a professor of computer science, human-computer interaction and design at Carnegie Mellon University, and coauthor of the *New York Times* best-selling book, *The Last Lecture*. Randy was diagnosed with terminal pancreatic cancer approximately one month before giving a speech titled

CHAPTER 15: HEALTH

"Really Achieving Your Childhood Dreams." *The Last Lecture* is a must-read if you want to keep health and happiness in perspective in your life. The book reflects Pausch's last lecture that he gave at Carnegie Mellon, which was a discussion about everything he wanted his children to know after pancreatic cancer took his life, since he knew he would not be around to teach them personally. A beautiful read.

So, let us discuss health and your success plan. I guess I should give the normal disclaimers here. Nothing in this book should be interpreted to be medical advice; you should always consult your physician before making decisions about exercise and nutrition.

I was always drawn to health and fitness, even as a child. That is one of the reasons I got into martial arts and decided to become a physical therapist. I have owned and operated a health club and martial arts academy for over 20 years. Throughout this time, I have seen thousands of people set fitness goals. Some obtained, but most not. I have seen every diet in the world and every type of fitness plan you can imagine. Everyone reacts a little differently to different programs, but I am going to briefly share with you what I feel the major components of a successful fitness program should be. This section is not meant to be the development of a specific plan, but rather a conceptual chapter noting why a sound health philosophy should be part of every success plan.

I intend to keep this section as simple as possible, because true health and fitness can be a bit like learning a new science, and would be beyond the scope of this text.

Most people think of health as their weight, but there is much more to it than that. In my opinion there are five pillars of health and fitness for us to address, and I am listing them in the order of importance. Take note that the first three reside in your head!

1. Spiritual

2. Mental

3. Social

4. Nutritional

5. Physical

SPIRITUAL:

If your soul is not healthy, then you are not healthy. I believe true health involves your soul, mind, and body being in harmony. Your relationship with your Creator is the most important health consideration. You need to have a deep and personal relationship with God to be healthy. Here are several ways to do this:

1. Spend quiet time with God every day. (Psalm 46:10: "Be still and know that I am God.")

2. Spend time reading scripture daily. (Joshua 1:8: "This book of the law shall not depart out of your mouth; but you shall meditate therein day and night, that you may observe to do according to all that is written therein: for then you shall make your way prosperous, and then you shall have good success.")

CHAPTER 15: HEALTH

3. Attend a good Bible-teaching church. (Romans 10:17: "So then faith comes by hearing and hearing the word of God.")

As your spiritual relationship with God grows, so shall your faith, and all other important aspects of your life. This increase in faith greatly reduces stress and fosters a positive outlook, which is vital to your health.

MENTAL:

Mental health often gets overlooked, but it is much more important than physical health. I know plenty of people who make bad health choices, but they are strong mentally and just do not worry or stress about anything, and they are living with vitality in old age.

Here are several ways to create and maintain strong mental health and most of these are covered in this book already, but we will reinforce them here.

1. Meditate: Learn to meditate and practice it daily. Meditation slows your brain and gets your conscious mind out of the way. It is the gateway to higher understanding. The benefits are numerous and proven. (Joshua 1:8: "Keep this Book of the Law always on your lips; meditate on it day and night, so that you may be careful to do everything in it. Then you will be prosperous and successful.") It is best to practice meditation with breathing exercise, as they are closely related.

2. Positive input: The world will give you plenty of negative input from the different media outlets and face-to-face encounters with negative people. You must put positive things in your head each day through as many mediums as possible, such as self-talk, incantations, internal and external affirmations, audio books, select social events, scripture, and music. This playbook is designed to teach you to do this naturally, so if you are following the plays in the book, you will be doing this already. (Philippians 4:8: "Finally, brothers and sisters, whatever is true, whatever is noble, whatever is right, whatever is pure, whatever is lovely, whatever is admirable—if anything is excellent or praiseworthy—think about such things.")

3. De-stress: Your brain needs some downtime where you can unwind and simply have fun. Just like your computer needs to be rebooted at times so it is true with your brain. Try doing something fun and relaxing at least one time every three months. (Philippians 4:6: "Do not be anxious about anything.")

4. Laughter: Laughter really is good medicine. You need to laugh often. Do this through finding appropriate comedic audio or video. Read funny articles. Make a funny friend or, in my case, just have a couple of hilarious kids. (Job 8:21: "He will yet fill your mouth with laughter and your lips with shouts of joy.")

5. Sleep: Restful sleep is imperative for everyone, but especially the high performer. I will never forget the advice

CHAPTER 15: HEALTH

a Korean tae kwon do grandmaster gave me when I was nineteen years old. He said that most people in America work and stay busy all day, only to have their mind do the same all night. When they wake up, they are no more rested than when they laid down. There is a reason so many are on medication in order to sleep. I am no sleep expert, but I personally believe there are several things you can do to learn to rest well.

a. Make your bedroom a sanctuary made for sleeping, and not a catch-all room where you eat, watch TV, etc.

b. Never have negative discussion in your bedroom or before bed. Save them for another time and place.

c. Do not look at phone screens, etc. within two hours of going to sleep.

d. Watch, listen to, think on, and speak of only positive things right before bed.

e. Upon lying down, do a mental "ramp down" of your entire body, focusing on your breathing. Start at your head and work to your toes, relaxing each body part. Any time your mind wanders, just bring it back to your breath. Do not try too hard. Most people mess this up by trying to be perfect. Just give in and do not worry about it.

f. If you have a lot on your mind, jot it down in a notebook and get it out of your head and onto the paper. Once you write it down let it go. (Matthew 6:34: "Therefore do not worry about tomorrow, for tomorrow will worry about itself.")

g. If you have trouble winding down on a given day, try walking barefoot outside in the grass for twenty to thirty minutes. There is something uniquely relaxing and grounding about feeling the earth under your bare feet.

h. Tell your Divine Mind that you want a healing, restful, and restorative sleep, and then see yourself sleeping comfortably.

SOCIAL:

The importance of positive social activity often flies under the radar. There are numerous research studies that support this. Some suggest that strong social connectedness may be the most important factor in longevity. This is one reason that a Spirit-led community church is often of great benefit. The love, fellowship, and support can go a long way. (Hebrews 10:24–25: "And let us consider how we may spur one another on toward love and good deeds, not giving up meeting together, as some are in the habit of doing, but encouraging on another—and all the more as you see the Day approaching.")

NUTRITIONAL:

There are three questions you need to ask yourself regarding nutrition.

1. Why am I eating or drinking now?

2. What is the quality of the food or drink I am taking in?

3. What is my input? (Number and kind of calories. We will address output in the physical activity section, but please note they are directly related.)

Let us take a few minutes to look at each question.

Why am I eating now?

Are you eating just to fill your belly, or are you eating for vitality? If you struggle with "diet," you are probably eating for the wrong reasons. Reasons such as trying to fill your belly, relieve boredom, relieve stress, or just being habitual. If you can take control of this question and only eat for vitality, you will be off to a great start. I prefer to eat four to six smaller meals per day, which includes healthy snack/meals based on my activity levels for the day.

What is the quality of the food I am eating?

I often use the following analogy to put food quality in perspective. You pull up at a gas station and find two pumps side by side. One states that it contains 100 percent pure, wholesome gas and the other states that it holds gas mixed with various chemicals and other additives that your car does not need. Which would you choose? Seems like a no-brainer, right? I think, even if the pure gas was more expensive, you would still select it over the low-quality option.

Then why don't you do this with your food choices? Most people would never choose the gas with chemicals and additives, yet they do it with their food all the time. We eat all types of processed food with chemicals that we cannot even pronounce. I am not saying that anything you cannot pronounce is bad for you, so if in doubt, do some research. The argument that I most often hear is that organic food is too expensive. My reply is always the same. It may appear that organic is more expensive on the front end, but if you consider the back end it comes out much cheaper. If you can prevent one disease, one medication, one doctor visit or one hospital stay, you will save plenty in the long run.

You must think about it this way. I believe the reason folks know better but still eat bad food is because they simply trust that if it is on the shelf at the grocery store then it must be okay. Most people think surely if it is allowed to be produced and sold it is okay for me to eat, but that simply isn't true. In my opinion, the food companies in America for the most part are only concerned with sales today, and not your health tomorrow. They market, market, market. They change a food's color, taste, and smell just to get it in your cart. Do not fall for it! Most all of nature's secrets are hidden away in organic fruits, vegetables, and meats. We may never know how all the macronutrients and micronutrients in these foods complement each other to affect our bodies in positive ways.

Your body is an amazing filter, but do not take it for granted. It filters through all the thousands of nutrients, good and bad, and tries to utilize what it can while battling the often-harmful side effects of the ones it cannot use. Help your body by making the right decisions on food quality.

I believe in eating a 100 percent organic, GMO-free diet. I even go so far as to try to grow or raise most of my own food or get it from neighbors that I trust to grow organic. It is true that the best diets are organic and possibly do not even include meat, although I do choose to still eat some meat. I do make sure my meat is organic for the most part.

CHAPTER 15: HEALTH

Here is a list of what I personally like:

- Organic fruits and vegetables
  - Try to include all colors

- Organic lean meats (You can cut meat all together or at least decrease intake)
  - If beef, I like a certified organic lean option to lower cholesterol and lower fat as compared to other beef choices.

- Wild-caught fish from mercury-tested waters.

- Organic plant and berry-based green drink (supplement) I prefer Living Fuel.
  - Must be harvested at the appropriate time and by proper methods to preserve nutrition

- Organic, plant-based protein supplement as needed. I prefer Living Fuel.

- **Pure water. (Not city water.) For most, eight to twelve, eight-ounce cups per day. Hydration is the number one health initiative! Research has shown that even a 2 to 3 percent decrease in water can decrease thinking proficiency and physical reactions.

- Organic nut mixtures

Superfoods that I like:

- Green tea

- Organic garlic (real or supplement)

- Organic apple-cider vinegar (real or supplement)

- Organic beet supplement (real or supplement)

I do want to give you a "heads up" here. Most folks that switch to organic foods feel a little weird for a few weeks as their bodies adapt to not having the chemicals and additives that they are accustomed to. However, after this transition period, they feel great.

What is my input? (number and kind of calories)

Input versus output: Put simply, this means, are you taking in more fuel than you are burning up? Think about it like a ten-gallon gas tank on your car. If every day you put ten gallons of gas in your car, and you only burn five gallons per day, then you will have excess gas spilling out all over the place. The only difference is that with your body, the extra fuel instead of running out, often spills over into fat cells, which leads to dreaded weight gain and unhealthy conditions. You should not have a problem with this one if you switch to an organic diet as the nutrition you will be getting will be of the highest quality and will be utilized differently. Proper nutrition will help regulate the input versus output equation in a positive way.

CHAPTER 15: HEALTH

Finally, the input question cannot be answered without causally relating it to the output question, which falls under physical activity which we will be addressing in the next paragraph.

PHYSICAL ACTIVITY
In a technologically advanced society, it is becoming harder and harder for folks to be physically active. Many of us have to be on a computer or at a desk for work and communication; plus our kids are doing five sports at once, so we are always sitting at practices and games for hours; and we get home to watch all of the TV shows that have been marketed to us throughout the day. If you think about it, years ago, our great-grandparents ate lots of fat and hopefully three square meals a day, but the difference was that they were burning most of it off through farming, chopping wood, and other manual labor tasks needed to survive. The main problem with the way life used to be is that the body usually gets out of balance and "overuse syndromes" usually developed with those repetitive activities that they had to do to survive. Any repetitive activity needs to be countered with an opposing stretching and strengthening plan, for optimal health.

There is no doubt we have slowly became a more sedentary and softer society, and I really dislike this aspect of "advancement." I will not talk about the "getting softer" subject, as it is too long, and would be a more suited topic for another time. The bottom line is that your body was made to move, and it needs to. I will never forget a martial arts student of mine who said, "We'll either wear out or rust out, so I'm going to keep moving." I love that saying, and I live by it.

Training and teaching Brazilian jiujitsu and MMA for over 20 years has given me my fair share of injuries, but when I compared myself to sedentary friends, I realized they were much worse off than me. They had chronic problems that never got better, whereas I could always bounce back. I do think there is a happy medium here; everything in moderation. Preventing injury is important. One of the worst things you can do for a vehicle is to let it sit for an extended period without cranking the engine or driving it. When you eventually drive it, there will generally be all kinds of new problems popping up. Newton's Law of Motion, which basically states that an object in motion is easier to keep in motion, is very applicable to your body. It is much easier to stay active as we age if we never stop being active to begin with.

When it comes to planning movement, I developed the "Five to Thrive":

1. Consistency: Get at least forty-five minutes of physical activity, six days a week, that at a minimum cause you to break a light sweat.

2. Variety: Change your activities every four weeks to prevent adaptation and overuse syndrome. I like to get outside and get healthy doses of sunshine.

3. Enjoyment: Find activities that you enjoy, preferably outside in nature.

CHAPTER 15: HEALTH

4. Comradery: Activities in groups generally make you more accountable, and you will often push your limits more. This group can be your family.

5. Intensity: Alternate intensity as appropriate, to stimulate different systems and muscle fibers. I do think there is magic in breaking a sweat!

If you struggle with weight or energy, it is a great practice to create a Daily Activity Log (DAL) with the following information:
   a. Date
   b. Time of day
   c. Duration of activity
   d. Intensity (scale 1–10, with 10 being extremely difficult)
   e. Perception (how you felt during and after)
   f. Estimated calories burned

You may not need to do this once you have developed the habit and are consistently on track with whatever goals you have set. This is a training aid, so you will have a record of what worked and what did not, so you can master your body.

There are three other things that I like to include when looking at the physical aspects of health. These are deep breathing, stretching, and massage. These three activities work in harmony to keep the body balanced and in harmony with the mind. Appropriately oxygenated muscles and organs, flexible joints and muscles, better blood flow, and mobile soft tissue go a long way toward optimal performance. The body was designed in harmony, and only the lack of proper activity or repetitiveness of the exact same activity interrupts it. The key with flexibility is consistency, mental focus, and patience. Massage is the fun part of this chapter. I know it can seem a little expensive, but like we have discussed, it may cost more on the front end, but will save you in the long run. The benefits of massage are numerous, so just trust me and get them as regularly as you can afford.

CHAPTER 15: HEALTH

Play 15
HEALTH

1. Make a list of several places that you can purchase organic foods and compare prices. Be sure to include local growers, where you can often see their growing practices and generally save money too. Try to make the conversion to an all-organic diet within the next two months. (Remember, most people feel a little weird at first until their bodies clear the old toxins.)

2. Write down everything you eat, along with the calorie amount, for two weeks, just to get a handle on how many calories you are taking in. Compare this with the estimated calories burned on your DAL and keep them in line with your goals. (Remember, if you are wanting to add muscle, you need to take in more "good" fuel than you burn. If you are wanting to maintain, you need to stay around neutral and if you are wanting to lose, then you need to burn more than you consume.)

3. Create your DAL (Daily Activity Log) to ensure you are including the "Five to Thrive." Be sure to include the following information:
   a. Date
   b. Time of day

    c. Duration of activity
    d. Intensity (scale 1–10, with 10 being extremely difficult)
    e. Perception (how you felt during and after)
    f. Estimated calories burned

4. List three unhealthy habits that you are currently doing, and eliminate them one at a time. Do not eliminate the second item until the first one is eliminated, and so on. (Remember, everything in moderation—you can have a cheat day.)

5. Start a stretching routine. Stretch daily, even if for only five or ten minutes. I prefer at least thirty, but just find a starting point.

6. Get massages as regularly as you can afford. Once per week, biweekly, once a month . . . or once every three months. Just whatever you can do, but do make this part of your strategy. Maybe you could trade off with a spouse, so you can help each other and keep the cost down. You will not be as good as a professional, but will be better than nothing.

7. Learn some basic breathing techniques, especially breathing for relaxation. There is lots of good information out there on this subject. Be sure to vet it appropriately.

8. Learn the basics of meditation. I was fortunate enough to learn meditation from a Korean grandmaster in

CHAPTER 15: HEALTH

martial arts and then furthered my study afterward. There are plenty of good teachers around, but again must be vetted appropriately. My best advice here is to not make it more complicated than it is. I like Dr. Joe Dispenza's work.

CHAPTER 16
GRIT

PHILIPPIANS 4:13: *I can do all things through Christ which strengthens me.*

JAMES 1:12: *Blessed is the one who perseveres under trial because, having stood the test, that person will receive the crown of life that the Lord has promised to those who love him.*

PSALMS 1:2–3: *. . . but whose delight is in the law of the Lord, and who meditates on his law, day and night. That person is like a tree planted by streams of water, which yields its fruit in season, and whose leaf does not wither—whatever they do prospers.*

Isiah 41:10: *So do not fear, for I am with you; do not be dismayed, for I am your God. I will strengthen you and help you; I will uphold you with my righteous right hand.*

Psalms 28:7: *The Lord is my strength and my shield: my heart trusts in him, and he helps me.*

2 Corinthians 12:9: *But he said to me, "My grace is sufficient for you, for my power is made perfect in weakness." Therefore, I will boast all the more gladly about my weaknesses, so that Christ's power may rest on me.*

"Nothing can withstand the power of the human will if it is willing to stake its very existence to the extent of its purpose."
—Benjamin Disraeli, British politician and writer

"Where the will is great, defeat succumbs."
—Kevin Pyles

"Success finds those that have the grit to stay the course."
—Kevin Pyles

Probably all of you have heard the saying that it is not how many times you get knocked down but how many times you get back up. Although I believe this statement to be true, I will attest that it is much easier said when you are up. I also think it

CHAPTER 16: GRIT

important to know what you will do differently when you get back up, so it will be less likely to happen again.

Grit and willpower go hand in hand. Grit is defined as courage, resolve, or strength of character; willpower is the trait of one's strength in controlling one's own behavior. In my martial arts academy, I teach the kids that the most important stance they will learn is the "ready stance." This is where the child must stand perfectly still with their hands clinched to a fist in front of their belt. The reason this stance is so important is because it shows that the child can control himself or herself. If they cannot control themselves here, then they cannot control someone else in a self-defense situation or a competition. Without this skill, they will not be able to control themselves as needed to learn any new skill.

You would think this would be easy, but it is not. It is nearly impossible for kids to stand perfectly still for even one minute. (Adults too, for that matter.) I have noticed that it is worse now than it was 20 years ago. I think kids are so used to being stimulated, they just do not know how to "be still" with no external stimulus. They eventually get it, with a lot of hard work. I try to drill the importance of this stance into these kids. If you visit my academy and hear me yell, "Ready stance shows what?" you will hear the class answer in loud unison, "Self-control!" Then I will yell, "Self-control is your ability to control, who?" and the class will answer, "Yourself!" A lot of adults could benefit from hearing this every day, as they often have the same problem. It may not be in the form of standing still, but in the form of staying on task day after day with no oversight.

It is imperative that you develop grit to ensure you stay the course to success, no matter what that course puts before you. I mentioned this earlier in the book, but it warrants stating again. I believe that many adults get stuck in what I call "puppy phase." See, puppies are only thinking about the moment. They simply react to the environment. They bite, chew, pull the leash left, then right, with no purpose or intent. They have not a thought of consequence or future. A puppy will chase its own tail, if there's nothing around to stimulate it.

There are a lot of people like this, too, they just hide it well. I had fighters that would be trying to cut weight for a fight, and they would come to me and say, "I just can't cut the weight, Coach. I'm working my butt off, but the weight just won't come off." When I would stop by their house to see how they were doing there would be a pizza box, junk food, or beer cartons in the trash. See, they simply did not have the grit or willpower to stay the course. In the beginning, it helps to surround yourself with other gritty people. I have had salesmen who miss their sales quotas, but never miss making a couple of social media posts during work hours. It is all about willpower.

So just why is willpower so elusive? I think there are several reasons, but one of the main ones is that it is never developed because it is never taught or never practiced. Many research studies claim that grit or willpower is like a muscle; it must be developed or built up, and that there are several factors that lead to this, such as values, belief systems, moods, and attitudes. Like a muscle can get fatigued, so it is true with willpower, and once you are fatigued, it is easier to give in. I would have some really tough guys that would fight MMA, but once they got tired in a fight, they might as well have been a 10-year-old kid, because they just wanted out.

CHAPTER 16: GRIT

There is no shortage of research studies that support the theory that willpower can be depleted. One of the leading researchers on willpower, Roy F. Baumeister, PhD, a social psychologist at Florida State University, goes in-depth on this subject in his book *Willpower: Rediscovering the Greatest Human Strength*, coauthored with journalist John Tierney. In his book, he describes surprising evidence that willpower is a limited resource, subject to being depleted. For example, in one study, he invited some students to eat fresh-baked chocolate-chip cookies, and asked others to resist the cookies and eat radishes instead. Then he gave them exceedingly difficult geometry puzzles to solve. The students who ate the cookies worked on the puzzles for about 20 minutes, on average. But the students who had resisted the tempting cookies, gave up after an average of only 8 minutes.

Such studies suggest that some willpower was used up by the first task, leaving less for the second. They have found that the "decision-making muscles" also deplete willpower. Armed with this information, it is important not to tempt yourself at the times when you are willpower-deficient. Just like the physical callus your skin builds up when you expose it to repetitive hard work, you need to develop a mental callus, a willpower callus. You can only do this by developing a strategy. It is important not to overestimate your willpower, especially in the beginning. For example, if you used to drink a lot of alcohol and you do not want to drink anymore, it is probably not a good idea to hang out at bars on Friday nights in the beginning.

I am certain that on your path to success, you will want to give up more than once. In fact, every successful person that I have ever talked to has told me about a time when they just wanted to quit and throw in the towel. You must develop a belief that success is right around the corner. A belief of "I do not know when I'll quit, but it will not be today."

I have had MMA fighters and jiujitsu students, who at the beginning, would give up as soon as they got stuck in a bad position or became fatigued; but after months of hard training and mental conditioning, you would have to nearly kill them to make them quit. As you continue to make the daily decision to keep yourself on track, you will get better and better at staying on track, and eventually it will be impossible to derail you. One of the best ways to support your willpower is to have clear reasons of why you must succeed, along with a continual reminder of those reasons.

Willpower is all about discipline. When most people hear the word "discipline," they associate it with being restricted or limited, but in truth, discipline equals freedom. You must stay strong and never give up. You must not be denied. Successful people do not have anything that you do not, they just never gave up! Believe me, you have what it takes!

CHAPTER 16: GRIT

Play 16
GRIT

1. List three things that truly test your willpower. Pick one at a time and practice using your willpower to resist. Once you have mastered one area, you can move on to another.

2. Take special note of anytime that you fail to stay the course, and write down the variables. You will begin to see patterns of what depletes your willpower, and where you may have holes in your game. Then you can begin to build and strengthen your willpower to an unbreakable level.

3. Reward yourself. When you have used your willpower effectively, try rewarding yourself in some way. You earned it!

4. Get gritty and disciplines in the small things. Make it a way of life, a belief system, and soon you will have grit in the large things.

CHAPTER 17
GIVING

2 CORINTHIANS 9:6: *Remember this: Whoever sows sparingly will also reap sparingly, and whoever sows generously will also reap generously.*

DEUTERONOMY 15:10: *Give generously to him and do so without a grudging heart; then because of this the Lord your God will bless you in all your work and in everything you put your hand to.*

1 CHRONICLES 29:9: *Then the people rejoiced because they have offered so willingly, for they made their offering to the Lord with a whole heart, and King David also rejoiced greatly.*

PROVERBS 11:24–25: *There is one who scatters, and yet increases all the more, and there is one who withholds what is justly* due, and yet it results only in want. The generous man will be prosperous, and he who waters will himself be watered.

PROVERBS 21:26: . . . *the righteous gives and does not hold back.*

MALACHI 3:10: *"Bring the whole tithe into the storehouse, so that there may be food in My house, and test Me now in this," says the Lord of hosts, "if I will not open for you the windows of heaven and pour out for you a blessing until it overflows."*

JOHN 3:16: *For God so loved the world that he gave his only begotten son, that whosoever believes in Him wouldn't perish, but would have eternal life.*

MATTHEW 6:3–4: *But when you give to the poor, do not let your left hand know what your right hand is doing, so that your giving will be in secret; and your Father who sees what is done in secret will reward you.*

LUKE 6:38: *Give, and it will be given to you. They will pour into your lap a good measure, pressed down, shaken together, and running over. For by your standard of measure, it will be measured to you in return.*

ACTS 20:35: *In everything I showed you that by working hard in this manner you must help the weak and remember the words of the Lord Jesus, that He Himself said, "It is more blessed to give than to receive."*

CHAPTER 17: GIVING

I purposely included a lot of scripture here, because this is often a topic that is not as readily grasped. There is no question how our Lord feels about giving. I believe the secret of giving is not just in the good deed itself, but in the way it makes you feel. It de-stresses you, it humbles you, and it motivates you. As a new Christian, I started to tithe but did not understand its true power. Through our walk with God, my wife and I realized the more we gave of our money, time, and talents, the more blessings we received both internal and external. God makes this clear in his teachings. Giving is not only good for the receiver, but also for the giver.

I think the biggest mistake that people make is they think they should wait until they "make it" before they begin to give. This could not be further from the truth. If you do not have money, then give of your talents or time. The benefit is all the same. I honestly believe the more you give, the more you receive, and I am living proof of that. This is not just in money coming back to you but also opportunity and people's talents and time. There are not many success courses or books out there that talk about giving your way to success. But this book is based off scripture and meant to be all encompassing. My desire was to include all the principles that it takes to be not only successful but also happy and fulfilled. I do not believe you can be successful and happy in your heart without giving along the way. The more you make financially or the more time you have of your own, the more you can do for others. So, everybody wins!

"You will never regret having given, but only failing to give."
—Kevin Pyles

It is important to keep in mind that the amount you give is in direct relation to what you have to give. A person giving 5 dollars of their total of 15 is much more gracious than the person with 100 dollars giving 10. Jesus taught this. You cannot out-give God. It is simply impossible. All that you have is owed to Him. He gave his only Son to save you from your sin. When in doubt—give.

CHAPTER 17: GIVING

Play 17

GIVING

1. Make a list of five places that you can give either one or a combination of:
   a. Your time
   b. Your talents
   c. Your money
   d. Your stuff

2. Start giving one or several of the above once a month. Be sure this is not only to people you know, but also to those you do not know as well. You will find soon that once per month is not enough and that you desire to do more. Be ready, because the blessings will begin to flow!

3. Write down what you gave and how it made you feel. Even if you do not reference it often, this will be a treasure to the family and friends you one day leave behind. Having a journal like this to read will be a true gift and a great example to the future generations of your family.

CHAPTER 18
CELEBRATE

PROVERBS 17:22: *A cheerful heart is good medicine, but a crushed spirit dries up the bones.*

PHILIPPIANS 4:4: *Rejoice in the Lord always. I will say it again: Rejoice!*

JAMES 4:13–15: *Now listen, you who say, "Today or tomorrow we will go to this or that city, spend a year there, carry on business and make money." Why, you do not even know what will happen tomorrow. What is your life? You are a mist that appears for a little while and then vanishes. Instead, you ought to say, "If it is the Lord's will, we will live and do this or that."*

> *"Celebrate the small successes to ensure you are there for the big ones."*
> —Kevin Pyles

> *"The more you praise and celebrate your life, the more there is in life to celebrate."*
> —Oprah Winfrey

You must celebrate the process of success. Life is about the journey as much as it is about the destination. Celebrating the process will ensure that you are living now and not just preparing to live. Things change, bad things can happen, and loved ones pass on, so do not stay on the "someday" train. Celebrate the small milestones along the way.

This is not just because celebrating is fun, but it makes you happier, which, in turn, will make you more effective. Rutgers University psychology professor Nancy Fagley performed a study where she had nearly 250 undergraduates take a survey measuring their levels of appreciation. Fagley's survey of appreciation focused on eight aspects, including awe, defined as feeling a sense of connection to nature or life itself and living in the present moment. The focus of the study was to determine whether appreciation carries distinct happiness benefits on its own, regardless of one's personality or level of gratitude. Fagley found that appreciation and gratitude both seem to be strongly connected to happiness. However, her results suggest that appreciation is twice as significant as gratitude in determining overall satisfaction with one's life.

I think there are often two extremes: those who never stop and smell the roses and those who stop and pitch a tent. You must

CHAPTER 18: CELEBRATE

have a balance of celebration and hard work. One of the many things that attracted me to my wife was that she always made me aware that I needed to be smelling the roses more. I really struggled with this in the beginning, until I learned more about the importance of celebrating, through my studies of success.

I like to think of the success journey like a professional MMA fight. First you prepare yourself by learning as much as possible from great teachers, then you put yourself out there by showing up on fight night. The bell rings and give it your all for five minutes. Then you get a one-minute rest where your corner provides water, tends wounds, and gives some encouragement and strategy. This one-minute feels like a slice of Heaven but it will not last long. Just when you start to catch your breath you hear tap . . . tap . . . tap, it is time to get back in the fight! Your success journey is like a fight that never ends. You will have hard rounds, and easy rounds. You will have rounds that you win, and rounds that you lose. You will get knocked down, but must get back up and change your approach. You cannot rest too much, because the next round will be waiting. Your coaches and family will be there to "fix you up," so you can continue. There will be times you want to quit, but you must stay in the fight. Some fights will take all the tools you have, and put your fortitude to the test. Stay in the fight, and you will win! This is why you must enjoy the process. For example, if you are in sales and you want to make $150K per year and you are currently at $30K; don't wait until you get to the $150K before you celebrate, because you may burn out before you get there. Set some small goals. If you make an extra 100 calls per day for 4 weeks straight, then take a day off and take your spouse somewhere nice. That is celebrating the process.

I will never forget a story I had read about how kamikaze pilots had to live. Each day they would meet to see which pilots would be flying the next day. If it was your time, then you knew that today would be your last day to be alive. One of the pilots was noted as saying, "You must plan like you will live forever, while knowing that you may die tomorrow." What a powerful statement. Think about how they must have felt. A pilot could be skipped over until the war ended and have a long life which they needed to be prepared for, or on the other hand, they could be selected tomorrow, and their life would be cut short. Hopefully, most of us will never be in a situation quite like this, but what a good way to live. Prepare for the long-term, while living in the moment.

One of the best things I did many years ago was to add the words, "while living in awe" to every one of my written goals. This is a constant reminder that I had to stay connected to life and enjoy the small things while working toward my goals and you should do this too.

CHAPTER 18: CELEBRATE

Play 18

CELEBRATE

1. Go back to each one of your goals and, at the end, add "while living in awe."

2. Define ahead of time what small achievements along the way will trigger celebrations, and then stick to it. Remember, it does not have to only be for "wins" but can be for process achievements, like doing a task consistently for a certain period.

3. Make a list of the people such as family, friends, employees, and customers that it will take to help you achieve your goals. Be sure to develop a plan that celebrates them along the way. Remember, it is only lonely at the top if you did not take people with you along the way!

CHAPTER 19
FINAL THOUGHTS

In closing, I would like to reiterate that every winning player must do several things:

1. He must surround himself with the best coaches and players.

2. He must know how to play and win the game.

3. He must implement and run the best plays consistently.

4. He must focus on the fundamentals.

5. He must constantly evaluate the effectiveness of himself, his plays, and his fellow players and react accordingly, while never changing the end goal.

6. He must celebrate the process along the way.

7. He must be willing to learn, grow, and improve.

8. He must be grateful and gracious in victory and defeat.

9. He must love the game and the players.

10. He must never, never give up.

Read this book several times. Be sure to create a special binder to contain the plays. Run the plays exactly as described. They are tried and tested!

I am confident that if you do this, you will become the fulfilled, successful, and prosperous man or woman you were destined to be. You will achieve your dreams and experience success and happiness beyond your imagination.

Lastly, please be sure to pass the teaching on to your children, so they can pass to their children. Start them at a young age; they are much smarter than you think. My greatest desire is that all God's people experience life as He meant for them to.

Now, go create your destiny!

"Believe in yourself today to have tomorrow believe in you."
—Kevin Pyles

ABOUT THE AUTHOR

Kevin is a successful, Christian entrepreneur currently owning and operating multiple thriving businesses. He is also a licensed physical therapist, Brazilian Jiu-Jitsu Black Belt, motivational speaker, and rancher. His passion is to help Christians find their way to success and happiness. He and his wife Derina have three wonderful children, Carmen, Kage and Kaleah.

Kevin has studied success and personal development for over 30 years, but it has not always been that way. Moving out of his home at only 16 years of age, he soon found himself living in an 8 x 10 camper where he realized something had to change. Going from desperation to inspiration, he began a relentless quest to achieve success, scouring through thousands of books, seminars, and eventually scripture. Everything he learned has been self-tested and either kept, improved upon, or discarded. After developing a specific and proven methodology to success and fulfillment, he wanted to leave a written record for his children to follow and thus The Divine Playbook was born.

He has mentored and guided many to their own life of success and everyone says he has a gift of making things simple and actionable. You cannot help but be motivated after you talk with him. He has an unstoppable, positive attitude that is contagious, and we hope you catch it through this book!

Follow him on Parler @kbpyles

Follow him on Facebook at https://www.facebook.com/kevin.pyles.96

www.ingramcontent.com/pod-product-compliance
Lightning Source LLC
Chambersburg PA
CBHW030905080526
44589CB00010B/157